Unhealed Wound

Unhealed Wound

Lorenbelle

To order additional copies of this book, contact:
Xlibris Corporation
1-888-795-4274
www.Xlibris.com
Orders@Xlibris.com
111274

I was born and raised in a WE tribe as we commonly called it in the West of IVORY COAST. In that tribe, the cultural values of the tradition are not only the sources of wisdom and knowledge, but also the basic rules of a long lasting marriage life

The WE tribe was formed by the immigrants from LIBERIA during the colonization. They established in the west part of the IVORY COAST back of the years 1889. The WE tribe social culture and values are based on their variety traditional masks, initiation dances; baby showers celebration after the baby was born, wedding celebration, the circumcision celebration, ritualism and the celebration of life after death.

According our ancestors, any marriage without the parent's agreement is not approved by God. In the WE society, the marriage is always a process of investigations. The bride and the groom' families members must be well known by the community where they socialize.

Both families must have a good relationship with people of their community. Sometimes both families can be from different tribes, but it doesn't matter where come from because people will always investigate about the person that they want their son or their daughter to be married. Some of us even before we were born, we are already engaged without knowing our future husband. At the early embryonic stage, we are engaged if we are born as a female by chance; and we will get married to the man that the family chose us soon we grow up.

In those tribes, the conception of marriage is based on a close and trustworthy relationship between families. No matter how you feel about yourself after you have grown, and whosoever you think you will be married to, must be a dream because your choices are unspoken. Your inner conscience in term of love in a marriage must be forgotten because it doesn't have any room. What matter is your submission, and the most important things are the honor and the reputation of your family's members. Your own glory and emotions are nothing but your unborn dream therefore You have to say goodbye to your better tomorrow. Your own existence is based on the obedience to your society's rules and principals for your respect and your safety.

Those rules, principals, and regulations of the tradition not only take away your pride without your consent, but also make you look as "a juicy fruit without flavor".

To tell the truth I love the tradition, its cultures and rules of regulations, though those traditions make you denied your own personality and your birth right as a female, but they are a powerful tools of learning concepts, and they established a basic foundation of peace and mutual respect for one and other. They guarantee the long life relationship between the community members.

In any society of this hearth, cultures and traditions always impact human being's life whether positive or negative.

As one of the Ivorian famous writer AMADOU AMPATHEBA said "When an old man died it is the whole library that burns" That means the elderly people are knowledge and wisdom carriers in AFRICAN societies. AMADOU AMPATHEBA's statement was related to the past. Before the colonization, all AFRICAN traditions and cultures were orally spoken not written. The only person who could remember the past and tell the truth of our ancestor's lives were the elders. "LE GRIOTISM" We called. It was the way to tell the history of our ancestor's coming from and their civilizations by a series of songs.

Knowledge and wisdom are the keys of the zeal in African societies. That for sure I can't deny it and I always approve it. I'm an example of those rules and principals of teaching and correcting a child for his socialization, the respect of others and good conduct throughout his life time. Regardless where I may be today, or whom I may be living with, or what I may be tomorrow, I will always be comfortable with my environment, and I can cope with any situation that I may go through. That my way to reflect the image of my dearest AFRICA. We learn how to fly or to solve our problems by ourselves without our parents.

At my work sometimes people ask me how long I have seen my family. When I tell them that I have seen them more than four years, they shout saying how can you deal with? How do you do to stay away from your family so long? I was brought up in that way, I have to get used to any life trials without my family no matter how. We are initiated to be bold and courageous at any cost, so we can face life on our own, and take our destiny in our own hand.

Nevertheless, thought I love my tradition, even though it helps me to grow on my own for a better socialization, I think that exception should be made through out time, because of the social cultural interferences and interactions of the new generation educational background.

Yet, those discussions about the moderation of the African societies, their principals of living, their rules and perceptions of life are out of question in some tribes. According to the elderly people, African society will died if we new generation give up to our traditions and cultures. We will never know who we really are. I may say yes, I agree on that statement, but every society must give up at certain time trough out life changes to its own concept of analyzing or seeing things in another perspective point of view. I know that it not going to be easy to sweep away all the roots of those traditions and cultures.

The interference of religions and cultures should be one of the factors of the culture changes, but some tribes still don't want any civilization from the far country as they are called.

As an example my great grandfather was a Mandingo immigrant trader from GUINEE CONAKRY in WEST AFRICA. He established in Ivory Coast back of years 1891 looking forward for prosperity. He was a very handsome man said my grandmother, and polite to all the chiefs of the county where he was established. His commitment and hard work made him become famous within few years in a region where he was living. His faithfulness to the chief of the land, granted him a huge favor. They gave him more land and some servants to work for him. He married more than 5 fives. Some people because of the good friendship that they have with my great grand-father gave their daughters in marriage to him. He was the point of contact of business for every village surrounding him. His place soon became a village market caring out his name everywhere in the county. "GBANHINBLY" That means the village of multiplication. As matter of fact my great grandfather had numerous children and a lot of wealth.

My mom's was born from a royal family. My great grandfather from my mom side was a king. He divorced my great grand mom from her previous husband, reimbursed her bride price three times because of her beauty then remarried her and toke her first born who was a boy as his own son. She was the only wife that my great grandfather had as wife and she his unique love till he died. Together their have my maternal grandfather who was his first born as a prince, and two other beautiful girls. They have a light skin and very beautiful as their mom.

It not only in African societies that the King has a power to do what HE wants, or chooses whom I wanted to choose, But the rules of the kingdom and its principals are applied to all societies regardless their denomination. The KING is always the sovereign of the kingdom therefore he as power over every decision that he want to make for his good or for the good of his people. My great grandfather was neither Christian, nor Mulsuman, but animist.

In my father's family we have both religions: Mulsuman and Christian, but we do not have any problem living or sharing together what we have for the well being of the family. I can tell that everything was ok regardless our religion diversity. When I was 8 years old, I used to spend some times with my paternal grand mom. During Ramadan, the fasting month she always teaches me how the woman should take care of her husband, and how to cook. We got up early in a morning to prepare the meal. We used to do everything together. I know that if she was still a life I would have get married to a Mulsuman. She always makes me dressed with those long nice young Mulsuman girl dresses. She implied that the way a respectful woman should be dressed is to cover her entire body.

I loved my maternal granny. Every time we have the school vacation I will use my tuition money and buy a head wrap or a traditional blue eyes liner for her. I was also her favor granddaughter because the family named me after her mother in law the GUEEN Another reason why she loved me so much was that I listen to her, and always help her to do her house work. Every time I go to my maternal village I'm always welcome with a royalty honor. All that I do is to make myself beautiful in a morning and wait for my meal.

All the women in my mom's family will take turn to cook for me until I live the village. My aunt Helen will collect all the meals and asks me to choose the one I want to eat. She will also put water in a shower for me soon I woke up. Uncle Edouard always offers me a rooster when

I'm about to live the village. I adore my mom's family that the reason why I always visit them any time I have chance to do it.

In Africa some communities named the baby after someone closed to them, but already dead. We call it reincarnation. People always come back to life after they died. It was a tradition, before the baby was born, the mother or the father will have a dream and the person who wants to come back to life, will reveal himself through the mother of the baby, or through another person in a family. It may be strange that a dead person comes back to life through another living human being, but that is the truth. IN African societies the dead always live among us. Sometimes if the dead person who wants to come back to life did not reveal it before the baby was born, he will show some signs to make himself known. IN case the mother or the father don't dream about anything to determine whose name the baby will have, they will go to the native doctor to know whose name the baby will take. That's how I was named after my great grand mom. Since I was named after my great grand mom the Queen everybody called me by her name. It was an honor for me to be called by the Queen's name and be her heritance.

To me having a solid economic support from your family doesn't make any difference for who I'm. I want to be myself. I want to achieve my own goal with a personal effort. All that I wanted was to go to school. Education was the key of the real freedom as a woman to me. Being educated as an African woman was an achievement for me. I did not want to be like my mom who despite her smartness never had that opportunity to go to school. My dream was to be a political leader one day when I finish my studies. I want to be part of the government members one day before I died. I have to give back something to my country to be proud of myself. I was a very smart kid, a brilliant girl at a primary school. I loved to study and had the desire to learn more and more from everybody.

My older brother Paul who is now an UNATED NATION ORGANIZATION (O.N.U) police officer I, and some of my cousins, we all were attending the same primary school of the neighbor village. The location of the school was about one hour and half from our village. SEABLY was the village were the school was located, and GBADROU was our village which was about 50 mile from the school. Sometimes my brother and I go to our mom in our father's village called ZIONDROU. Every day we go back and forth from Monday to Friday except Thursday which was our day off from school. We never complained about the distance of the school. In fact we enjoyed the ambiance and the interaction between us and the students from the other village. Everything was perfect to me. I loved being part of that type of scholastic environment. It did make learn a lot from other and gave me the strength to be self confident.

My primary school teacher's named MR. EMILE GOULIA. A very straight forward man. I really likes him because he made us learn a lot. He will beat you up and punish you if you don't learn your lessons before you come to class. You will write hundred times on one of his paper that you will learn your lesson before you come to school. One thing also is that we are not supposed to communicate in or mother's tongue. We must communicate in French. If just by mistake you spoke your language, one of your class mates will report you to the principal. And that day, they will put a big bone of a cow on your neck till you give it to somebody else. If nobody ever spoke the mother tongue for the rest of the day, you will keep the bone until they found another person to take it away from you. I remember going home one evening with the big bone on my neck because nobody took it from me. The next day I have to bring it back, but it was on my neck until I passed it to another person. From that time I never spoke my language for the rest of the year was very happy to go to school. Every Christmas eve my cousin Denis TIELA's mom cooked for us and bring it to school for the holyday togetherness before we dismiss school. The school requested that even each year for the students family's fellowship. It was recommended that every family should cooked for their children and bring it at school, so all the kids can eat together. I always love that moment of togetherness, because it was the only time that we see our family's members, and our classmate family's members around us and putting their meals together to eat with us.

One of the things that I did admire was our courage and our determination to go to school. Most of us came from different villages far away from where the school was located, and every morning we have to travel back and forth. Despite our tiredness, we always enjoy fighting against one group and another before we reach our destination. The physical fight was a real pleasure for us. Each village must show his potential of power. One day, one of the fighters headed my brother Paul. Before we reached the village, my brother's right eye couldn't be seen because it was all swelled up. I was so worried about him, and I was telling the student who bit him that my mom will show him who she is when we get into the village. Soon we reached the village I run without stop to the house and tell my mom about what just happened to my brother. My mom quickly, jumped from her sit and run toward my brother Paul to see how bad the situation was. Soon my mom saw my brother's eyes; she screamed of anger and pushed me away furiously telling me to get on her way as if I was the one who did it. Who did this to my son? She asked me. I told her who did it and how everything started. She grasped my brother by his hand, and quickly went to see the boy's family. I will show him front of his parents how good it is to have your eyes like that.

Everybody knows my mom in a village. Her nickname was a police officer. She doesn't take any situation as easy as you will think. If she says that she will show the boy how good it is to have your eyes like that, she means it. I was running behind her. When we were going to see the boy's family, some people by curiosity follow us to see what is going to happen. The boy's father soon he saw my mom coming, run toward her and kneed down begging her to take it easy. He called my mom by her nick name saying: <Tiassi, Ditokoua.> my sister let us solve this matter as a family please. I will take your son to the hospital tonight. He told his wife to give his hand bag and his shoes that is going to call the cab. That night they took my brother to the hospital. My mom and Uncle Edward went with cab driver. They came back from the hospital around midnight. The good thing was that the cab drivers always come to the village at any time. The village wasn't far from the city, and some people who work in a city live in a village. They go in a morning to the city to work than come back at night. That really helped the villages because in case of an emergency like my brother's it easy to find the remedy of the problem.

It was all having fan even though we got hurt sometimes. There was no day that we don't fight before we reached the village. Each day that we come to school is different from another because you don't know what will happen, but one thing sure you always have to be ready when an unexpected occurred. Through those daily fights, we all learned how to become warriors. I really did like that type of school life because it teaches you how to count on yourself in time of troubles. The other thing that I like too was the weekend. Saturday was the market day, and we don't have school afternoon. That day everybody is happy because our parents will come to the market to sell their products, and we will have money to buy what we wanted to buy. Every Thursday we don't go to school, and that day my brother Paul will use it to make his bamboo helicopters or build a bamboo houses for his collections. My brother Paul was genial building toys houses or a toys plane. Sometimes he will sell them because they so beautiful people just want to buy them. Life in a village was peaceful and lovely. How I wished I could stay in village for another school year, but unfortunately my primary school year in a village did not last longer because of my father's cousin uncle Jule.

My child wood was a little bit rough I did not grow up with my mom when I was child. I was adopted by my father's cousin Felicity who did not have a child. She was a register nurse in Abidjan the capital of the Ivory Coast. After she passed away we went back to the village for the burial that was the first year that I spend together with my mom. After my adoptive mom's funeral, I have to stay in a village for my first primary school year.

My first primary school year was very shot because my dad's cousin uncle Jule took me back to Abidjan one month before the summer vacations end up. Soon we reached Abidjan, he went to sign me up for another primary school for my second year. It was one of the best school in one of the city square called TREICHVILLE. The school named ECOLE du POND The school was called like that because it was located just after the bridge. Every morning I have to take the bus by myself to go and come back night time. The first time that I went to school by myself I got lost. I was so shy I did not tell the bus driver that I had to get down after the bridge. I reached school that day at 10am. As time goes by, I got used to everything. I was feeling comfortable of doing things alone. On year later, my mom came to visit me. I was very happy to see her again. I wished that she can take me with her to the village, but I have to stay and finish my school's year. So far everything was going perfect with my school until I graduated from the primary school. After the primary school graduation, it was summer vacations, and we are going back to the village. I was very happy because I will see my mother again after 5 years. For the vacation Uncle JULE gave some money to his wife Antoinette to do our chopping. Aunt Antou as we always call her, was a very sweet woman, very caring Uncle Jule and her had only one daughter, named Chantale. A very beautiful girl with big brown eyes, and a very light skin, she is just pretty as you can't imagine. In the house we were five girls, and we are all cousins from my father's side. Beatrice, Therese, Mariam, Chantale and myself. We are all cousins, but we have a different age.

Uncle Jule as all African man at that time had another mistress named Collette. He had two kids with her, one boy and a girl who just looked like Chantale their half sister. They all look just like uncle Jule and they are beautiful. In the square where we lived all the boys knew me because I always fight with them, and I beat them all the time. One day they all came in agreement to pay me back while I was at a market, but that was a big mistake because they lost the fight. I was so happy to go home with victory, but I did not mention anything to my ante Antoinette and my cousins because uncle Jule would have teach me a lesson since he gave me a warning for fighting with boys. The city square where we lived was called <QUQRTIER LATIN> It was one of the small square in ABIDJAN, but very niece and calm the square was built during the colonization by the FRENCH. The population of QUARTIER LATIN was a variety habitant from many nations.

He was the only one who had a woskwasguen at that time in a square were we lived. He never allowed us to be part of any party with our friends. We always cry, and begged ante Antoinette to let us go to a party, but she can't because uncle will beat her if he comes to know about it. We have to find our way to go to party anyhow. We all knew that uncle Jule never come home before 2am because he always go to his mistress before he comes home, so when we have a party, we come in agreement to pay someone to watch the door for us, and the person will let us know when uncle is coming home. His Woskwasguen had a unique sound at that point when uncle Jule is coming back home everybody knew that it was him. Soon the person who is watching the door tell us that uncle Jule is coming home, we run to the house right away to hide ourselves under the covers with our dresses. As nothing had happened we all started snoring. Soon he put his feet in a house he will start calling us one by one. We have to pretend that we are sleeping to avoid trouble. Nobody in the house told uncle Jule that we go to party sometimes. Whosoever gave him that information will be in trouble because uncle Jule will tell him that he is the one who took us there. Everybody knows what was going in the house when uncle is absent, but nobody will volunteer to say anything. They don't want any problem with him.

I remembered one New Year the model of the dresses we chose, was those classic style with a big holes in a middle of your chest which shows your breast from both sides. The material was so beautiful he bought it for all of us, and the style we chose was the one all the young girls worn at that time. Believe me we made a huge mistake sawing our dress like that. We were all well dress, ready to go out for the New Year when uncle Jule arrived.

What a "hell" I'm seeing get off those dresses that you have on, and put them on a table before I open my eyes he said.

He added: I did not buy you a cloth to put you breast out and show to every young man that you are ready to get married.

He was a Taylor himself, so he took our dresses one by one and sown back the hole between the breast. We all cried and refused to go out for the New Year. I went straight to my room and stay in bed for the rest of the day, so my cousins. He gave us a containers each one telling us to fill them with our teas otherwise, we are not going out for two days until he gave us a permission.

While I was crying, my cousin Chantale came to me and said: <Oh my God we better stop weeping now because it not possible to fill those containers don't you think so?>

I was so made at her that I told her to get away from me with her stupid way of thinking. I knew that she was telling the truth, but she is always like that. Anytime we have a situation going on, she will blaspheme and that is it you forget what you were about to do. She is never serious about anything for CHRIST sake.

My cousin Therese liked to fight a lot with me even though I always beat her, but after the fight we become friends again. Therese came to me and said: <hey grand mom today we are a big looser for this new year, let us not fight again and we have to try to understand each other from now and on.> I stared on her and tell her to get out of my room and never show her face again to me. She run away and went to Chantale to tell her what happen to her. Now they all came in a room to see me, stood by the door and said with a loud voice.

Come on grand mom let us forget about this dress. We have some other cloth that we can put and look much better than that one. Le get dress before the day is over please? Don't be hard on yourself let go girl.

Ok I get dress they all screamed and jump till the roof. We took our old cloth and went for the New Year's party to uncle FATOMA MIchel.

Aunt Antoinette used to sell fish at a market, every Thursday morning around 2am we have go to the fish market at the port by the Atlantic Ocean to get the fish the cases. Once we come back to the house, we will clean the fish till 5am in morning, than she will fried the first portion that I have to take to the market at 6am. I will stay at the market until 6pm and I come back home.

Those years that I spent together with my cousins were the best one If I can say. I always miss my cousins, and we never get chance to see each other until uncle Jule died.

Summer vacation started already and uncle Jule and I must park our stuff for the village. We have to travel with the public transportation, and the city where we are going is about 6000km from the capital. It will take us one night to reach there. The journey will be very long, and we all will be tired. It was Friday night around 8pm when we left ABIDJAN for the village.

We arrived Saturday morning let say 6am at MAN our home town. We have to take a taxi to go to the village. I was very much exacted to see the village, and the whole family member that I haven't seen for more than five years. All the family members were important to me, but the most important person was my grand mom. My maternal grand mom was everything to me, she was my role model. I never like to stay too long with my mom because she was very straight forward. everybody in a village like my grand mom because of her kindness. Sometimes she will cook, and save it thinking that an unexpected visitor can come from one moment to another. Some women in a village, sometimes came to her when they had visitors, and asked grand mom if she had something to eat.

Grand mom was born twin, but her other sister did not survive after birth. In my tradition when a woman is married, and go back to visit her family if something happened to her while she was there, supposed an accident happen to her. She has to be replaced by one of her youngest sister because her bride price had been paid already to her family. So it shall be. My maternal grand mom had to replace her sister to get married to my grandfather because her big sister who was married to my grandfather had an accident when she went to visit her parents and got paralyzed. She was only 13 years old when her sister who was married to my grandfather had an accident while she was in her family for visit. At 13 my grand mom replaced her sister. She was too young to understand love, but no comment on that. Love or not she has to go. Since my grandfather was a prince there was no problem for that. In fact it was an honor for her to be married to a prince. After the matrimonial ceremony, her family took her to my grandfather's village. Once in my grandfather's family, she will grow up and perform the circumcision ceremony when she will be 18 years old before my grandfather consider her as his legal wife. Grandmother MATOMA was lucky because my grandfather never ever took another wife. Despite his royal title he decided not to take other wife to add to my grandmother. People tried to convinced him to marry another wife because she was young, but he refused to do it. He said that his father the KING never married another wife besides of his mother so it shall be. Instead he became the first Christian protestant in a county, and gave up to his royal throne for his half little brother that his mom had before she got married to my great grandfather the king TROPKAHE.

My grandfather TIA was the only boy among two girls. He was a very handsome man, he had a beautiful white teeth, and he was neither tall nor shot. He was friendly to everybody in a village. I always miss my grandmother and my grandfather, and I will miss them for long. Before he died he asked to be buried by the protestant church of the county. No royal honor was given to him because that was his wish. Grandfather was an amble man he loves to share with all his family's members what he had. Even if it did not have enough, he will always give and share.

The summer vacation was great. My other cousin called Nitani Therese and I party from village to village every other Saturday, but we never end the party because uncle Gaston will always come to look for me and take us back to the village. Every night we joined the young girls from the village to gather in a middle of the village at a moon light to sing our favor song. summer vacation came to end, I started worried about my returning to school. I still do not know who was going to take me this time for the rest of my schooling. For curiosity I asked my mom if I was going back to uncle Jule. She replied that her brother Gaston BAH and his wife Yolande are going to take me with them. I felt relieve even though I never been to uncle Gaston because it was my first year in a college, and I don't want to miss my school year.

It was a tradition of the WE tribe that before your children go back to school, you have to make sure they have at least the provision that they may needs for the year. For that reason, my mom always has to be ready for us Mom gave us some of the new rice crop and red oil and some money. I never care about money when I was growing up. Anytime mom gave us money I gave it to my brother Paul. We will leave the village within two weeks. Now my happiness of going to school became an anxiety because it was my first time to go to uncle GASTON. I overheard that he was very straight and don't play around when it comes for girls, or for your education. All the same I'm happy at least someone will make sure that I study and pass my classes each year I like that. It two weeks already and tomorrow we are living the village early in a morning for KATIOLA one of the northern state in IVORY COAST. My mom and my grandmother, spent the night in my room just to give me some advises before our departure. I could sleep enough I was waiting for the night to be over. At 5am in morning my mom and my ante Helene uncle Edouard's wife started cooking our meal. We have to eat and the elder of the family who was my grandfather has to give us his blessings before we leave the village. At 1oam we started saying goodbye to all the family members.

As I was talking to my grandfather I saw the taxi driver puling over the house. He came to give us a ride. I remember that my mom was crying while putting the food in cab trunk but I was happy to go because I knew I was in good hands.

The journey was as longer as the very first one that I took when I was coming from the capital to the village. We left the city at 1pm and we made our first stop at 4pm in DALOA. One of the famous city in a west because of the agriculture grope abundance. We took 30mn of break and back to the road again. Our next stop was BOUAKE the capital of central, and it was 1am next day in morning when we arrived. I was very tired of seating but all the same happy to reach my destination pretty soon. After 45mn of break we left BOUAKE for KATIOLA wish was our final stop. KATIOLA was a very beautiful northern city. It was well known because of its political involvement, and one of the veteran wars named General THOMAS DAKIN. General DAKIN was a very powerful man very straight forward spoken person. In that City the black magic power is as easy as drinking a water. If you come across someone you better behave before you found yourself in a very critical health situation that can send you to your grave. People from that city can stop the sun or the rain if they want because of their supernatural power. People don't steal in that city. If you do it, your hand will stack at the item that you want to take till in a morning and everybody will know that you are a thief. I love KATIOLA not only for the fresh and natural food products, but also for its multiple academic schools, and it beauty. The first year that I came to KATIOLA, my uncle was living in a town not in a college, and my school was 3 min away from the house. I always wait the second bell of the school to ring before I leave the house. At my second year my uncle had a house inside of the college.

The college was composed of a boarding school for males and females of every age and every level of education. The administrators authorized to leave inside of the college were: the principal, the vise principal, the director, the under director the supervisors and the accounting. It was a big college with 24 classes two big refectories 36 dormitories, a tennis court volley ball court a big theatre center and a ball room. Each dormitory was supervised by the student who most has a better grade in the whole schooling year. In my second year I became a dormitory supervisor. My co-supervisor was a little bit older than I, but we pretty much understand each other because of our political motivation. I was also one of the leaders of the student political party movement calls M. E. C. I for a few years

I was really doing well at school, and my goal was to finish my school with good grades and be an honor student. My dream was to become a leader of one of the political party movement. One day to plead for the needed I'm for the social and I cannot close my eyes on a social discrimination toward the middle class. I advocated many times for the students and confronted my school administrators in presence of General THOMAS DAKIN. The abuse of the administrator's power over some female student for sexual harassment was common at that time. I signed a petition against them and sent them to the governor of the city. For that rebellion matter, the General THOMAS DAKIN was called by the governor to be present at the meeting. Believe me if I was wrong confronting my administrators for what they have done, my schooling year was over. My curriculum was done; I would have never attended any other school anywhere in my country. Thank God that all the investigations result was on my favor. The General DAKIN and the governor EMILE CONSTANT BOMBE openly congratulated me for my courage. They told me that the type of student that I' m has a long way to go and a may be a good party leader in a future.

As I was enjoy my schooling years focusing on my goal and my dream, I realized that will be 18 years next few months, and I'm supposed to get ready for a senior college, and 3 years later I will go to the National UNIVERSITY in a capital ABIDJAN. I did study very hard each year to make my dream comes true. I always have my scholarship each year. I never failed any of my classes because I wanted to keep my scholarship. All my energy and thought were driving toward my determination to succeed in a future. The only that attire my attention was my school.

The last and only thing that I can think about was my engagement with Vincent. For me being engage to someone or been married will drive away my dream, because what comes after the engagement is a wedding. I always avoid men because I don't want to be pregnant and give up to my school. If it happened I will go back to the village to get married like the young girls in a village. I always fight with boys when they expressed their love to me. To me having a relationship without finishing my studies was out of question. The ministry of Education's regulation was that any female student who gets pregnant is not supposed to attend the school any more.

As matter of fact one of the boarding school was pregnant and nobody knew about because she hided herself all the time. She used the shower room when nobody is not there because she doesn't want to get undress front of anybody. On her due day, she got up early in a morning around 4am went to the new building in construction to give birth. After giving birth, she thrown the new born in a pit of the bath room and came back to the dormitory as nothing. The baby was discovered three hours later by one of the girl who was passing by the building. The fire department came to get the baby out. The mother not only can never go to school, but she went to jail.

I was just afraid to attach myself to someone and give up of my ambitions. All the boys in a boarding school were my best friends I called them my children even though we have the same age. I was use to them and some of them we go to my family sometimes for vacation. They teach about men and women, when someone really loves you what and what he does. That was an advantage for me to know who man really was.

For my family time has come for me to belong to someone, but to whom should I belong? I have no idea since I wasn't dating anybody. All that I had on my mind was my achievement at school that was it nothing else.

It was too late for me because I can't think about going to school. My parents have already decided to marry me to the man of their choice. Vincent was an awesome young intelligent fellow. He saw me grow up while he was going to school because he was staying with uncle Gaston.

As the summer vacation was approaching, my cousin Bernard who was attending another college wrote me a letter. Vitamin B12 was the nickname given to my cousin Bernard. Bernard always has a severe chest pain, and the only medication that made him feel better was a vitamin B12. Any other medication couldn't cure him. In his letter he said: "Hey grand mom guest what. This vacation will be your engagement event with Vincent uncle Blaise's friend who is at UNIVERSITY in ABIDJAN. So get prepare MRS Vincent see you next". Soon I read that first part of his letter I never went further with a reading, I stopped and started shaking all over. I remember that day I didn't eat for the rest of night. I could figure out why uncle Gaston can act as he has never been to school. I did not know from where to start and from where to end. So many questions came across my mind but no answers for now. I know my uncle once his made up his mind he is fixed, he will never listen to anybody. Because of his economical power in a family no one can't confront him for any situation. Whatsoever decision that he took must be final. What could I tell him to change his mind about my engagement with Vincent? One thing that I know is that my mom is an agreement with uncle Gaston I have no doubt for that. I know that my uncle loves and he wanted me to get marry to an honorable and wealthy man like Vincent. My mom also I know how she loved to be glorified by people. She admire me all the time saying that one day I will get married someone who we treat me like a queen because he will have money to do it. I really don't understand my mother she has plenty of money. Every year she gives loaned people money to pay their children school fees, and they gave her back with interest. Why can she desire a wealthy man to be her daughter's husband? Goddamn I wish I would have been like some of my friends in a village, or like my youngest sister who refused to go to school and had her baby at 15. If my mom is involved then I have no chance at all to win the fight. I know my mom she is not an easy gum to chew.

I tried to share the topic with some of my dormitory mate to get some advises from some of them. It seems like my entire dormitory mate approved the decision made by my family. One of my roommates asked me if Vincent was huggle.

No I replied

Does he have a good job?

He just got his master in law and the government gave him a scholarship of two years for the Law School in Paris I replied

So what is your problem he will be working pretty soon, and you will become the high class first lady she added.

First lady I replied. I rather be a last low class lady with a little bit of feeling in my heart for the person who is supposed to be my husband.

Do you mean that you don't love him at all? He has a lot of potential to be pushed away from women don't you think so. She asked

Wait a minute you are talking about love? I never dated him I said. He saw me when I was growing up here in this city while he was at a college that all. Sometimes he and my junior uncle sent me to buy a soda for their girl friends when they come over uncle's house.

I never had him on my mind. Actually he is the last person that I could think about.

Hey who is talking about love. Do you have to love him? All you need is his title and his money in a future to achieve your goal and your family's goal she said. She continued saying that now day love doesn't matter. The most important thing is money and government power. Aren't you happy when people look you as a luckiest one to have a husband judge than any man as an ordinary woman like everybody else?

Yes because I want to be a first class lady I have to get married without any love in my heart.

I will not go for it. No way I will not. Maybe over my dead body. I just can't believe that people will act in 20 century as if they never been to school. What is wrong with them? What I coming over my uncle? I'm done with all of them done for good. I was so upset so "piss off" that I started shaking and crying hiding my face between my palm.

Cool down she said. You need to seat down with your family and let them know that what you want from them is to support you for your studies.

Would I be able to face my uncle? Who is doing everything for me? Is he going to listen to me and let me achieve my goal? I don't think so. I wish I can have someone to get me pregnant and that is it.

Do you have anybody in your mind? Who can do that? She asked.

I wish I can scream and let everybody know that I need a man who can take my proud before I give myself to Vincent. Yes I wish I could my dear roommate.

Do you have any other uncle where you can go for this vacation instead of staying with uncle Gaston? It will be good for your peace she said.

I think a have my father's cousin in a capital I can go there for my vacation.

Here we are solution has been found. You see sometimes it good to talk Loren belle.

I know Kari, but I wasn't thinking going anywhere. I never go to people except uncle Gaston and his wife Yolande.

Each vacation uncle will always send a message to my legal guardian. He will recommend him that I have to live the boarding school two days before everybody. Soon my legal guardian received the message; he will make a request at school for my leave of absence. The next day he will put me in the car to go to my family.

Since I knew what my uncle had in his mind, I decided to take an action and figure out what I have to do.

Before uncle's message reached my legal guardian, I must be gone to Uncle Etienne my father's cousin. I will not need help from anybody for my transport because I always work hard to keep my scholarship so I did not have any money problem to travel. I don't need anything from anybody before I leave the school.

That day that I had a conversation with my roommate, I was very sad the whole evening. During the night I could sleep. I was waiting for the day to come so I can leave as quicker as possible.

All my stuff where already park a head. I just want to go far away from here.

Early in a morning after the breakfast, I told my roommate that I was ready to go to the bus station. She volunteers to go with me to the bus stop for my departure.

She and I were never closed as we are now even though we share the same dormitory. But she was very concerned about my situation because she knows that my refusal to marry Vincent would cause a conflict between me and my parents. I wasn't ready to give up to my fight no matter how, and that worried her too much.

Before we dismissed she told this.

"Never give up on your dream and goal no matter how hard and traumatic the situation between you and your family may be. I have faith on you Lorenbelle you can make it."

We both were in tears while we were hugging each other to kiss goodbye for next year.

Finally we looked each other and started laughing.

Sheer up and I wish you a good and safe journey see you in October she said.

Thank for everything. I really appreciate your support I said to her.

It was Friday in a month of June when I left KATIOLA for ABIDJAN. The bus station was crowded of students going for vacation all over the country. There wasn't a cell phone like now to call my father's cousin and tell him that I was coming to him for vacation. I would have wrote to him one month ahead if I knew that I was going to stay with him, but my decision was taking at a last minute. Uncle Etiennn and his wife Mary are going to be surprised soon they see me coming. It was my first time to go to them, but I was glad because everybody talks about Uncle Etienne and his wife kindness.

I know that I will be comfortable once I'm there. As I our journey was about to end, I started thinking about how I was going to enjoy my summer vacation. It wasn't my first time to be in the capital, I was there before when I was an adolescent with uncle Jule, but not since I have grown.

It was 12 pm when we reached our final destination to the city. I was so tired and angry at the same time, but I have to use my last energy to look for a cub and go home. Soon the taxi pull over Uncle Etienne came closer to see who was coming to his house. As soon he set his eyes on me he jumped on my neck to hug me. That is my niece; my favor niece he was saying to all his neighbor. He was so exacted to see me. Right away he paid the driver and took me to the house. You must be tired, go take your shower I fix you something for you to eat when done.

He could wait to ask me the good news that brought me to him. While I was eating I explained the reason why I came to see him. He told me with a peaceful voice: "My daughter you have come to your father, and I will not allow anybody to torment you." After I ate we discuss for couple hours then I went to bed. That day I was so exhausted that I did not know when his wife came home. I must be in a deep sleep when she came back from work that night. In a morning before I got up she was already gone to work. Uncle went later, but before he left, he wrote me a note to let me know where he put the money and I can go to the market to cook if I wanted. I got up around 10 am that very next day. After I took my shower and got dress I decided to go to the big market square. I did not take the cab I took the short cut between the houses. On my way to the market after quarter mile of walk I met a young fellow on top of the hill. I did not know who is at a very first place when he stopped me. He looked in the eyes chook his head.

Who are you? I asked.

Of course you cannot remember me beautiful young lady he replied.

He took more than half hour before he introduced himself to me.

FRANCK was the nickname that people used to call him. He was my brother's classmate when we were in primary school in a village. I was never closed to him because he wasn't in my class. He was the first who stopped me and reminded me that he was my brother's classmate at a primary school in a village.

My goodness you have grown up. I had no clue that I will see you here in this city with my own eyes. That is beautiful to have you here with me. He said

Where do you live? And with whom you stay? He kept asking me.

With Uncle Etienne and his wife I replied.

OH that genial your uncle lives just close to me. He went to work isn't it?

Hum . . . yes why do you ask me this question? And why are so happy to see me? I asked him.

You were too young at that time to understand what I was feeling inside of me on your behalf he added.

Oh really what you mean by that? I though you said that you know my brother Paul I asked.

Nothing I let you know later because I will come to pay you a visit tomorrow. He said

Visit me for what? I told him that I just arrived to the city, and it my first time to stay with my uncle I don't want any trouble. Please let me be I don't want you to come to my place please.

Ok I know what you saying, but this time I'm not going to let you go or loose you again. I will be there tomorrow with my brother Joe at 10pm to see your uncle he said.

Are you serious? François waits a minute you just don't mean it I said to him.

Do you think that I'm playing Mss Kossa? Of course I'm serious he replied.

Oh my God from one trouble to another what can I do? Can you wait at least two weeks after my arrival to come to our place?

I was so anxious that soon my uncle came home, I did not hold to my peace to tell him everything.

Oh he thinks that he is going to be around my niece any time that he wants? Let him come and see me. He will found himself in a prison for the rest of his life said my uncle with hunger.

He doesn't know me I will show him "pepper" uncle emphasized. In IVORY COAST when we use that type of idiom, which means the person who is coming to you must be prepared because it going to be a misunderstanding. Sometimes end up with a big fight.

I was so scared when my uncle was expressing his hunger feelings, but his wife turn around and caressed my shoulder telling me that everything will be ok.

You know your uncle loves you too much because you made him pride at school. And he will not let anybody mess you up with your school. I will tell him that nothing will happen to you. It's not going to be easy for me to make your uncle understand that you will be fine. You know that your uncle is very jealous when he sees a young man close to you. Like all good fathers he is protecting his daughter she said.

I was quickly relief when I heard those words of comfort from her. Without wasting my time I asked her: Aunt Mary do you think that uncle will let me come for vacation again if François keeps doing this?

My daughter don't worry your uncle will be happy to see you hundred times here for vacation she answered.

As night was approaching, my heart started beating faster and faster. I can stop thinking about everything. I wish François did not show up just for today. I was very quiet. I could not even hear the noise of the TV because my mind was far away from where I was sitting. All my thought was focused on François and his Brother Joe's visit. I could stop checking on my wash to see what time it was. It was 9: 45pm oh God don't do this to me please let them come some other time not today I said to myself. As I was saying goodnight to my uncle and his wife to go to sleep, I head the door bell ringing. My uncle went to open the door since he already knew who was coming. I pretended to ignore the visitors and went straight to my bedroom. Lay on my bed I overheard my uncle asking Joe what good new brought them to him tonight.

I have been your neighbor for many years, but it never crossed your mind you and your brother to come and visit me. How come my niece is here today and you come to visit me? He questioned Joe François's brother.

One proverb said that" the hunter always follow the traces of the deer before he shoot." Said Joe

My dear friend, we are here to visit you because we need your help. But for tonight, we just came to say hello to you and your family Continued Joe.

Ok my family and I welcome you and your brother François in our house said my uncle.

Thank for giving us your hospitality, may the God of our four fathers bless you François's brother JOE said.

Amen, so you said my uncle.

As a tradition required, when you have someone in your house, you have to offer him something to drink. My uncle offers them liquor and some beer. All the moment that François and his brother sympathized with my family, I was in my room. I wasn't allow to come out without my uncle's permission that our tradition.

Now that I know the reason why you came to visit me you came go back to house because I don't need your presence in my house for this moment. My niece just came I need a time with her. She is not looking for a husband for now.

Couple hours later, Joe asked to leave." My brother and I must go home now, but we will be back some other time my friend" he said.

Ok it was a pleasure to see you Joe. I wish you and your brother goodnight, and hope not seeing you again.

Thanks, and see next time said Joe to my uncle.

I did talk neither to François nor to his brother Joe until they left the house. I stay in my room till next day morning.

Two days later after they came to my uncle, François came back to see me. My uncle and his wife were at work.

We can't see each other François because my uncle is not home. Don't come to visit me when they are not home. I don't want any trouble with my family please I said to him.

You see I can stay one day without you. I think I will give up to my school and look for a job so I can be able to provide whatsoever you may need he said to me.

No Franck I called him. You can't abandon your school because of me. Don't do that because I'm not ready to get married yet. You see the reason why I escaped to come here, is because uncle Gaston want to married me to Vincent.

Which Vincent my cousin who is at UNIVERSITY? He asked me

Yes, but how you guys are related? I asked him.

Vincent mom and my mom are from the same family he replied.

My paternal grandmother is from that village of your mom too I mentioned to him.

I know but your grandmother and my mom are not related, so we are not blood cousin he said.

Ok François but please do not give up to your education for me.

Despite my disagreement of visiting me whether at my uncle presence or not he never stopped to come to my place. Sometimes we will go to movie and come back before my uncle comes home.

Day by day week by week François and I started dating behind my uncle's back. For the all month of summer vacation Francois and I were together. I did not tell anything to my uncle, but it seemed like he knew everything that was going on. One night he told me that we are moving. Uncle bought a house far away from where François lives. That square was called TOIT ROUGE the house was in another area of the city. It was new square the houses were built by the government and people and people just buy them. They were very beautiful houses, but that area was empty because of the bushes people were afraid to live there. The compound was totally closed you don't see your neighbor when you are in your compound. At that time we were the second family to establish in the area. Before we definitely moved I went to see François, and I let him know where my family and I are going to stay. Any how he can't come to see me there because my uncle will put him in jail. In AFRICA the abuse of the administration power has no limit. If you mess with someone who has a friend who can put you into troubles, you surely will be in trouble. That how it works. Be in a relationship with high class personality is all that it takes to put someone behind bars. My uncle was trying to do what he could to put François and me apart from another, but we always see each other somehow.

I was having fun on my summer vacation putting behind me my engagement issue with Vincent.

My heart indeed was in peace because Uncle Etienne will not allow such of wedding, and I wish I could have stay with him for the rest of my schooling year.

Time was flying, soon I have to go back to school, and all that worried me was uncle Gaston. He wrote to Uncle Etienne and told him that next vacation Vincent is coming to him, so I'm supposed to be in TIASSALE before night fall for Christmas Eve.

Uncle Etienne you sees what I was talking about. I will not go anywhere I said to him.

No my daughter you don't need to run away otherwise the situation will never end. You should go just obeyed and go to him. Pretend to agree with their decision, but you know what you have in your mind. Don't let them know that you are not happy for what they are doing. Even if Vincent is there with you don't show any sign of misbehavior.

What are you implying Uncle Etienne that I should date Vincent even if I don't love him? I just can pretend that everything is ok with me, and I'm not going to allow Vincent to destroy my life for his own good no I said

Would you listen to me? Did you hear what I said, or did you understand what I'm saying? Uncle furiously questioned me.

Yes uncle I understand what you saying I replied.

Ok then do what I said and stop tormenting yourself.

I only have three weeks left to go back to school. Summer was over Francois decided not to go back to school but to look for a quick job in order for us to be together.

He should not have done this to himself for my seek, but he did it because he wants to show my family that he is a responsible man, who can have a wife and give her whatever she may need.

One week before my departure to KATIOLA, I went to see Francois. I told him that we need to talk about our future, and if he is going to let me finish my schooling after we get married.

Why not, do I look like someone who is going to keep you in captivity because I will have money? Do not even think about it. Of course it will be my pleasure to have an intellectual woman as my dear wife. We are in a new society where woman have all the right to express themselves babe. So feel free to achieve your goal and fulfill your heart desire.

Thank you very much Francois for understanding me I said to him.

You are more than welcome sweet heart.

As François was talking, he put his hands in his right pocket, and handles me an urge amount of money, and said to me: "I have nothing to give you but love and comfort for now. Take that money whit you, you may need it when you get there. I know that uncle Gaston is mad of you therefore he will not buy your school items, so I bought them for you." I was really surprise and chocked at the same time. I asked him where he got all this money.

I work at a club as a server. Each vacation that I'm here I always work there he said.

Are you going to give me all your money? Don't do that please I have a scholarship every three months that I can use. Don't worry about me. You need that money too François. The reason why you work each vacation it because you need money for yourself too, so don't give it to me

No you mean a lot to me babe and you come first. I got enough money for all of us. Take this money if you love me, and if I'm special to you.

Ok I take it and again thank you.

You are welcome sweetheart.

I just can't believe that he can give me all this money. We are just dating nothing else, so why he is so kind to me. It the first year that we been together. He wasn't supposed to do all this for me, but he did.

Soon I get home; I told Uncle Etienne that Francois gave me some money.

How much did he give you? I hope he is not spoiling your mind. Who told him to pay all this for you? Did I tell him that I cannot honor my responsibility? Did you ask him any money?

No uncle I didn't ask him nothing. François just volunteer to help for my school

OK than tell him that I don't need his help said uncle.

Be happy that she is in good hands. That young man is very polite and responsible said uncle's wife.

I know how you women are said uncle to his wife. Are you thinking to give her in marriage to François as a wife isn't it? It was just an observation my dear husband. Overall what is a wish of all fathers? If it not for your girls to be married to a good husbands. A husband who can honor his responsibilities said Aunt Mary.

They both started arguing on my behalf without any agreement. I have to cut short and tell them that they have to stop fighting against one and other that everything will be fine. We need to focus on my luggage because I have to leave within few hours instead.

Couple hours later, we left the house for the bus station for my departure. I just don't know why I don't like to take the train. It would have been a little bit faster for a long trip like mine. The train makes only two stops before destination, but I still love to go by bus.

I did not want my uncle to give me a ride to the bus stop because he will not allow me to talk to François. So I whispered to my aunt to go with me. Aunt Mary was a very smart woman. She listens to everything that uncle said to her. She let him take over all the family's matter even thought she could say something. She knows my uncle so well. In fact they have been married more than 15 years. Despite their lack of agreement on certain issues, they love and cherish each other. Nobody can come between them. It was a true love.

Even after all those years of matrimonial they feel as if they just got married. She was very special to me. I always see her as my role model when I get married one day.

As aunt Mary and I were on our way to the bus stop, suddenly she asked me politely.

I can tell that you and François love each other isn't it? He is a good boy my daughter. We used to be a neighbor, and I know all the young men around this area, they are so unrespectfull, but François is polite and respectful everybody. He is a very hard working boy. He has no girl friend here in this town. So my niece that is it you have found a good looking and responsible man. Do not listen to parent, but follow your heart.

What my ante said was true François did not have any girl friend in a town. He was going to school to another neighbor country called TOGO. There was a woman that he felt in love with. Her name was Gertrude a very beautiful woman. He told me that he decided to marry her one day because he thought that he will never see me again. The day that he met on my way going to the market, he could take his eyes of me. He was asking himself if that was real. His long time dream of having me as a future wife came back to life. The first time that he saw me was at a primary school. Even though he never told me that he loved me, he always has hope that he will meet me one day as a grown woman. He said to me that he chided his feeling of love from me at that time because of my age. I was only 10 years old, and he had my oldest brother Paul's age." But his heart was telling him that one day I will meet me" he added.

Yes aunt I love François, but uncle Gaston and the rest of my mom's family want me to married Vincent. I really don't like the idea of getting married to someone that I don't love.

Now you are talking my niece, see in this life nobody should tell anybody what he should or shouldn't do. You have to follow your heart. François is giving up to his school and to his girl friend for you, don't disappointed him at all. He will fight for you and he will let you continue your studies. What I'm telling you my niece, is that life is a choice. Your uncle and I don't have a lot of money, but we love each other, and that is more than anything.

I think my aunt was right that the way it should be. Nobody should force anybody to get married without loving the partner. Though it our culture and tradition to be married without our consent we should fight against it. I will not allow such of thing to happen to me no.

My mind was made up during Christmas vacation, I will go to Francois. He is giving up everything that he had for me I can't pay him back like that because of my family.

François did not come to the bus station to say goodbye to me. He thought that my uncle will be there with me. But I told Aunt Mary to tell him that I will write him a letter soon I arrived at school. Ante said that she will let him know before she goes home. We kissed bye and I went straight to the car to seat.

The bus let ABIDJAN on Sunday at 6pm and reached KATIOLA the final destination Monday noon at 12pm.

Tired I was because I did not close my eyes all along the road. I always like to see everything trough the glasses when I'm traveling. I love to admire the nature and its beauty.

Soon I arrived at the boarding school; I throw all my stuff in my closet and went straight to take my shower. While I was in a shower, I overheard my roommate asking if I had a nice summer vacation. What are you implying Kadi? I asked.

Well it seems like someone had a nice vacations because you keep singing. Since you walked in the dormitory you never stopped singing and smiling. Tell me what happened during your summer vacation. Why are you so exacted? You are different Loren belle. You are not the same I used to know. You were never in such of good mood since your last engagement news. May I know the good news so I can help you enjoy?

I will tell you my dear friend. I'm more than exacted and more than happy. I'm the luckiest woman in this world.

I said to her that I think I'm in love.

She cracked and said to me: "Wait a minute what I'm hearing? Did I hear you saying love? No that can be I think you are dreaming Loren"

I replied to her and said: yes I'm in love. Is it a crime to be in love?

Hey, wow hold on to your peace. I'm just surprised that all. You Loren all you do are to study how can you be in love so quick?

Never mind who comes to you to manifest his feelings. You will turn him down now you talking about been in love. I'm glad that you are in love, but how are you going to do with your family? She said to me.

Now you got a point Caddie my dear friend. You see I don't want to be married to a chosen one, but the one my heart has chosen.

Who is that one? Kadi asked.

It François my oldest brother's classmate from the primary school.

What did he do for living? It doesn't matter to me as long as we love each other we will be fine love wins.

You see Loren belle you are looking for trouble. You know that our tradition doesn't allow such of foolishness. Your parents will not let you married Francois, so get over it and accommodate yourself with their decision. It for your good and you will be in peace.

Kari I called her. I can believe that you as an intellectual approved such of tribulation. I thought you were smart than I was, but I realized that was totally wrong. You don't even care about me. You don't even think that I have feelings that I need to express. No Kari I think you better than what I'm seeing. You have to set yourself free from those traditions and find your own way. You have to fight for the coming generation. We have to make our parents understand that life nowadays is different. Marriage nowadays is an agreement of two people who have to live together. It not just an order and only one yes is not enough to win. We new generation should come together and stand for the better tomorrow of our children and our Young sisters. As one voice we should cry loud, so the authority can hear us. They have to put a stop sign on forcing us to married whom their heart desire follows. I will not give up Kari. I will fight not only for my own seek, but also for my coming generation.

I hear you Loren belle, and I'm award of our feeling of love, but tell me what different can one cry make in a desert? As I'm talking to you now Lorenbelle, my wedding day is already set up for next summer vacation. I don't even know what type of color skin the person that I'm going to married has. I will know it the day of our wedding. The only thing that I know about him is that he is in EUROPE. His parents are my family's best friends, and since I was 12 years old, I was told that I will be his wife. I don't even know if I can focus on my studies because I don't know if I will go to school again after I have got married. I don't want my parent or my family members to reject me. All the same I don't want to stop my education. I have been thinking about everything Loren. My future, my classes, all my nights is like days because I can stop thinking about the pain inside of me. I have to scarify the love that I have for my boyfriend no matter how I feel. Our traditions are killers of love.

I have nothing to say that all I know Lorenbelle it a waste of your energy believe me honey. We both were in tears while we were talking to one and other. I felt Kadidia's pain because she is in a same situation as I'm. She cannot bear the weight of her anguish. When I look deep in her eyes, I can tell how much she wanted to get away from the situation. I know that it not easy to confront our parent. We can even discuss about the marriage topic with them. All we should do was to listen to their decision and obeyed.

I Lorenbelle will not take it. It doesn't matter what it will cost me to get what I want, but I will not say yes to them. I have my mind set up. This Christmas vacation, I will go to Francois let see what is going to happen.

Are you going to try your parent? Is that what you mean Loren? Don't even dare because you and François will lose your skin for life. Let us go get over it my dear friend. That is the last advice I can give you as a best friend.

The school year started as it always does. We had a lot of homework to do every week. The semester exam was at a same time. All the students should take the same math topic, geography, History, English, Spanish and French. Everybody was busy with a group of studies in order not only to pass your class, but also to keep your scholarship.

The school has a regulation that we have to follow all the time during the night studies.

During night studies, one student must supervised the class, and write the names of those who don't like to focus on their lesson review, but go around to talk to girls. They will be punished by the school principal later on. The rule was just applied to the students at a boarding school not all the school students.

The menus of the refectory were a variety component of meals. Each day the meal is different from another. We all have our favor meal. Sometimes we don't like what the kitchen offer, but since we have no way out we will eat with complaint. The college was far away from the city, and there was no convenient store around to buy something to eat when you are angry.

The boarding school student is not allowed to go to the city without the Administration's authorization. Before we leave the boarding school we have to report it to the Administration office, we have to sign a paper that we are on our own if something did happen to us.

Every Saturday we organized something to enjoy ourselves. Since we are not allowed to go to town we used one of the ballrooms to party. Sometimes we go to town without telling anything to anybody. We just go and come back before the refectory's hours. The reason why we have to come back during the refectory hours was that the supervisor has to call everybody while we are eaten to see who was absent. If you missed meals time, you have to have an explanation the next day to the supervisor's office.

We girls always covered our roommate if they refused to come to the refectory.

The school soon will be closed for Christmas vacation. Each student will go back to his families and come back after two weeks of break. We girls always make sure that we stay in connection with one another if we are from the same city. We were 5 days from the Christmas holydays when uncle Gaston sent a letter to the school principal who was his close friend.

He asked the school principal to let go two days ahead, because my fiancé Vincent will be coming from now and on. He insisted that the principal have to make sure that I took the bus whish goes to TIASSALE city where my family was living before he leaves the bus station.

When the principal shown me the letter that my uncle wrote on my behalf, I told myself that I have to the live the school before we dismiss. He did not say anything to the principal because I don't want him to know that I wasn't happy about my family's decision. Nevertheless He did ask me if I want to go the following day to my parents. He answered to him saying that I will wait until we have two days left. Soon the principal and I finished the conversation; I asked politely him if I could go back to my class. He answered "yes you can go my daughter I will call your uncle and let him know that I will do him the favor to put you in a bus for your departure".

Thank you principal I said to him then I left his office. As I was going back to the classroom, I started thinking how I will organize myself to leave the boarding school before time.

It wasn't an easiest decision to vacate the boarding school before our time. Now that my uncle has told the principle to keep his eyes on me how could I escape? That made my situation worse. Should I stay or should I go. Moreover nothing will change my decision to go to François. I had made up my mind that I will not give up for any reason. The fight must go on whether they like it or not. There is no back up I have to teach them a lesson once for good.

I was in class present physically, but I was totally absent in mind. I could wait for the teacher to dismiss so I go to the dormitory and get my suite case ready for tomorrow morning.

I was so miserable that I couldn't even eat when I went to the refectory. It was a night mare for me. My nights are like my days. I had a sleepless night for more than a week, and I cried under my blanket silently. It was a tradition for the entire boarding school student to talk to one another when it time to sleep. We always try to share something before we sleep. It could be a comment on our teachers, or a comment on one of the classmate. I was very quiet and covered my head; I bent my knees till my forehead like a sea shell.

Kadi realized my silence, and came to me. She sat on the edge of my bed. She put her hand on my shoulder and said to me.

"You are not alone I'm with you everything will be ok just promise me that you will stop torturing yourself. I help you tomorrow morning. Since we don't have class at that time you and I will take a cab to go to the train station."

Ok thank you Kadi I really appreciate your sympathy toward me. I will pay you back one day for all you doing for me.

Come on baby girl you don't need to thank me we are in a same boat for the fight.

Early in a morning I jumped in a shower in order to get ready before everybody got up.

I did not want anybody to know that I was going for vacation, so I told Kadi to take my luggage.

She is good helping people that are a gift God has given her. In any situation, anyhow, no matter what, she will come up with some ideas to save you from the disaster.

She went to stand at the entrance of the college to get the cab. She offered some money to the driver, and told him to go at a back of the dormitories and wait for us.

Soon the driver pull over I knew that it was the cab that Kadi went to get. Without asking the cab driver, I started putting my stuff inside of the car.

Is your friend Kadi who is traveling or you? The driver asked me.

Yes I'm the one traveling.

She is waiting for us on the other road where nobody can see you leaving, we are going to get her and soon your train leaves, and I will bring her back to the college he said.

Ok thank you Sir I said to him.

You don't have to thank me my daughter. You see I choose to be a Christian because of all these traditions that make you denied yourself sometimes. He continued saying that his first girl friend was from this town, but her family married her to someone else. She always send for him because she still in love with him. One thing our parents forgot is that love cannot be forced.

Yes you are right, but do they care I don't think so I replied.

So, tell me the man that your family wants you to married how old is he?

What type of job did he do? He must have a lot of money maybe.

He is at University, faculty of law.

Have you ever seen him?

Well he was living with my uncle when he was going to school.

H e used to attend the college where we are now.

So, he was a former student of your college

Yes he was they were the very first students when the college was open.

He is an intellectual man so why should he let himself abused by the tradition.

I have no say, and nobody wants to listen to me either. I wish I was born somewhere else far away from all this cultures, and have my own life the way it supposed to be. How I wished they can understand that things are changing therefore they should let their children to make their own choice when it comes for marriage.

Hey what I can tell you is to follow your heart not people. You are the one who is going to get married. If in a future the matrimonial doesn't work you are not going to go back to your family you know that.

Do you have somebody else in your mind? If so then go ahead with that person. If they come to know peace will be with you.

Hey I do that where I'm going now. I'm running away from all of them.

Poor kid may the LORD strengthen you he said to me.

Thank you I replied to him. He dropped me off with Kadi, and made a u-turn after me said goodbye.

It was 6:45 when I took my seat in a train. My heart was pounding because I don't want anybody from the school to see me living.

Soon the signal of the departure was given, I deeply breathe and said hoof.

My stress was over for now even though I have to face my parents later.

They will not even have a clue of where I should be unless I told them.

None of them has no idea that Francois and I did meet. The time they come to know the place where I went, my vacation will be over, and I will be at school already.

The journey was very long. From 6:45AM we arrived at DAOUKRO at 5 pm.

François knew that I was coming for Christmas vacations, but not so soon. I could call him because there was no cell phone back those days 80.

Despite my tiredness, I was very happy to be where François was. I felt in my heart he peace that I have been looking for. Mean why I was a little bit worried because I don't know if Francois was home that day.

I doubted of his being home because sometimes his job send him out of the city for couple days.

How would I manage if he is not home? Where would I stay until he comes back?

I didn't know anybody in the town it was my first time to go to him. I have some money with me, but it wasn't the routine to see a young lady like stay in the hotel by herself. How people will consider me. It was a shame for me to go the hotel alone. All kind of question was coming in my mind.

Soon I got down from the bus; I took a cab and give the address to the driver.

The nice side of the small city is that every taxi driver knows all the working class in the area.

While the driver was taking me home, I asked him if he knew the person who lives in the address where I was going.

Yes we cab drivers know pretty much everybody around here because we drop the art work every day. The young man who lives in this address named Francois, but we call him Francois. He is a very nice gentleman. I like him a lot sometimes he gives me a tip when I take him home.

Are you his wife I guest?

Why did you think that I'm his wife? I asked.

I just asked because since I have been dropping him I have never seen a woman in his house.

Yes I'm his future wife I said.

Ok Madame welcomes home, but did he know that you were coming?

No I came earlier than I was supposed.

You don't have a key for the house I think.

No I don't have it I replied

I will go to his work place to let him know that you are waiting on him.

I really appreciate your help SR, and I'm grateful for that.

I felt confident and relax after my conversation with the cab driver.

I removed my stuff from the taxi and gather them front of the door.

One hour later Franks came home.

He was very happy to see me. He could believe that I came.

He hugged me, kept me in his harms for couple minutes crying of joy and told me that he fought he was dreaming.

"Thank for coming, thank for doing this for me I love you with all my heart. I'm very glad that you make it to come. You can't imagine how happy and proud I'm of you"

You must be tired I know, so let go in. While you are taking your bath, I prepare you something to eat. You know what, I take you out to eat tonight he said to me.

After by bath I got dress and we went out to eat. The restaurant where we went was well known in a city for the quality of the meal and services.

After eating, we went back to the house. We sat in a living room to watch a TV and to talk about everything.

It was 8pm all ready he knew that I was tired, so he told me to get some rest for few hours before we go to the club.

Francois was someone who loved dancing a lot. Music was his passion not any kind of music but RAEGA. JYMMY CLIFT, ERIC DONALSON, and BOB MARLEY PITER TORSH all the Jamaican famous singer were in favor.

All the clubs are open from 9pm to 5am every Friday and Saturday night.

That night we had a lot of fun. He introduced me to his best friends as his wife.

I never had fun like that. All my worried was forgotten at that moment.

I put behind my mind the trouble that my family was given me. It wasn't question to think about anything that can make me sad or change my mood right now. All that I wanted was enjoyment and fun for my first night in a club.

I never drink and François will not allow me to do it. Everybody around me was having a beer, but I drunk coca cola or sprite. The food that we order was barbeque fish and a grill chicken pepper soup with atieke the national recipe of ground kassava and some fries rice.

That I felt as if I was in Heaven. Been in a boarding school is like to be in a prison. Even when I go to my family life doesn't make any difference because I will home until I go back to school.

I never had a chance to go somewhere with a friend or to do anything by my own without supervision.

My vacation was great I was very happy to be with Francois, and I will be back from now and on.

François and I were much closed, we understood each other, and we shared the same point of view. Life was very pleasant with him. We were really in love and nothing could have separated us. I was so busy doing a lot of thing that I did not realize that two weeks of vacation were already over. Within 3 days I have to live for school. I did not feel like going back there, but I have to because the school year wasn't over yet. I think François comes to realize that I wasn't in a mood to back. He said to me: "you know that your school is more important than anything I already gave up to school in order to work and let you finish, so don't give up too. Think about your goal and dream never mind what is happening with your parents, you should focus on your school"

Thank François for all your support; I don't know what I would have done without you.

You welcome babe Loren that why we are together, to help one and other. What a meaning of been partner if I'm not there when you need me who will be there for you.

I was encouraged of what he said to me. I was looking for someone who can be there for me. He knew what I wanted and what I needed. He understands me more than my own family, so for me François was the only person that I had for now.

The night before my departure, Francois took me to a restaurant where we went when I came to him. At the restaurant, he asked the bar tender to bring the food that he ordered.

While we were eating, he told me that he will be waiting for me during summer vacation.

Some of his co-workers came to join us for dinner. It was a very nice evening all of end up in a night club after eating. We came home around 4am in a morning. What a great night, I wish it never end, but unfortunately the night has to end to give way to the day light.

Two days later, we went to the train station to buy my ticket to go back to school.

It over I said to myself because I was supposed to go to uncle Gaston, and I came to François. Soon or later uncle will send me a letter to express his unhappiness toward me and my disobedience to him. It done I have to open a fight I'' bite their fingers'' as we said. I have to be ready for any matter that will occur.

Before I left François for school, we both made a commitment to stand firm on our decision of staying together. We agreed that no matter what happen we are not going to give up or to let one and other done. We sealed that promise, and we were not supposed to break it.

In fact I will be at school by tomorrow I remained myself. I don't know what I will expect from the principal who uncle Gaston recommended to keep eyes on me. I disrespected the principal therefore I don't know the outcome of my attitude toward him. I have to be ready to face my judgment follow by the punishment. Whether or not I have the right to do what I did, I will be punish for sure. Nor I have a comment to make about the situation neither I have to defend myself.

All the long of my journey I just couldn't stop thinking about my own dilemma. Coming back from my vacation I was very happy, but once I try to think about what was a head of me, my heart can't stop beating. I felt like shocking.

Ho God when will I be free from this stress? I asked myself

I wish my dad was still a life all this torture would have never happened to me.

I just can get my mind off of my engagement with Vincent. I felt like not going back to that school because I did not want to face the principal for what I have done. But shortly my journey will end and I have to face the reality of my dream.

It was 5pm when I arrived to KATIOLA train station that Sunday. Soon I got out from the train I called the cub driver for my ride to the boarding school.

After half hour of driving me finale reach the school and I told the driver to leave me by the dormitory. While was paying the cub, one of my roommate came to me and told that the principal was looking for me everywhere after I left the school. She added that he questioned Kadi my friend because he said that she knew where I was, but Kadi never told him anything. "I hope everything is fine with you when the principal comes to know that you are back" she said.

I know what it going to happen. No matter what I will be ok. I can handle it. I replied

Nothing has changed my mind regarding my opposition to be Vincent wife. Despite the challenge between my family and I was stronger than ever.

Around 8pm while we were in TV room, I heard a cab pulling over; I run out and saw that it was Kadi who was coming back from her vacation. I was more than happy to see her back. At least I have someone that I can talk to about everything. I was so excited to see Kadi than jumped out of the TV room and throw myself at her neck. She was almost about to fall down, but she was smiling telling that she was also glad to see me too.

We hugged over and over again at that point she forget the cab driver who dropped her.

Hey young ladies said the driver. I need my money so I can go.

Sorry my friend here is your money Said Kadi to the driver.

We took all her stuffs and went to the dormitory laughing. It was too late to make a noise because some of our roommate was already in bed.

It was a rule that after 8pm nobody was supposed to stay up. But some of us always make exception of the rule. Not because we are breaking it but we represent the administration that the reason why we have to sleep after everybody. We have to make sure that everything is ok before we go to bed.

That night Kadi and I didn't talk a lot. We went to bed after spoken few words to one and other.

As usual we all get up when the second bell rung. But I did not wait the second bell to get up because I wanted to be ready before everybody. Soon Kadi realized that I was up, she also got up and came to join me in a shower room.

Morning young lady Kadi said to me.

Morning princess I replied to her.

So what are you up did anybody told you that the principal was looking for you after you have left for vacation? Asked Kadi

Don't mention Kadi, Amy told me soon I came to the dormitory. I'm award my dear and I have to be ready for the meeting.

Don't tell me about said Kadi. She continued; the principal questioned me over and over again, but I insisted and did not change my answer which was no I don't know where she is and I didn't see her living the school.

What will you tell him if by chance he called you? She asked

By chance if he called me you said? I love you sense of humor Kadi I said to her.

What else you want me to say my dear friend Loren. She continued.

One thing is sure he is going to confront you Loren regarding your running away.

I know Kadi he surely will, and I'm trying to figure out what to say.

You don't need to hide the situation from him. Be open to tell everything LOREN and he will know how to help you.

Ok Kadi I will do exactly what you saying. The only topic that we discussed during the shower was my problem with the principal. We even forgot about the good time that we have during our vacation.

The principal usually don't come to the refectory during meal time. But that morning he came earlier than usual.

Everybody was surprised, and we were asking ourselves why he was there.

I could focused on my breakfast, I whispered in Kadi's hears and told her that I was living.

Don't you dear get up and attire his attention to you. She said to me. Let him do what he came for.

Soon the principal walk in our refectory, all the students got up to greet him.

He came to welcome back all the students, and congratulate everybody for their hard work which put the school at a very first place among all the schools in a town.

He gave a brief speech of encouragement and recognition.

Now I feel a little bit relax I can take my breakfast in peace.

Kadi looked at me and started laughing. I bet that you were almost going to have a heart attack isn't it?

Stop Kadi that is not a jock. You know how I feel about the situation.

Let us hurry up for class said Kadi. We need to be there before everyone to durst our seats.

That right I replied. We went quick to the dormitory to get our school bags and went into our classroom.

All the classes always start at 7am to 12p and we will be back for the second part which starts from 3pm to 6pm. Each day we have 8 hours of lessons. It was the first day of class since we came back from our CHRISTMAS holidays. Everyone was busy telling his own story about how he has spent his vacation.

The first day of school after holidays is always excited. Everyone is happy after visited his family.

Another excitement after holiday is that we always come back with some money giving by our parent for our needs. We have to do our best to keep that money until we receive our scholarship from the government. We get a scholarship from the government 3 times a year each 3months.

We were on Monday tomorrow is Tuesday, but I'm still thinking about the principal, because he hasn't call me yet. How I wish to meet him and get over the situation between him and I.

It has been 3 day since we came back from vacation, and I haven't encountered him yet.

I told myself that I will not think about it again, but Friday morning while we were on our break, the supervisor came to me and handled me a letter. Nothing was written on except my name. I opened it and starting reading it. It was only two lines of phrases wrote by the principal telling me to see him during my afternoon break. I put the letter in my pocket and went straight to class. Kadi hasn't come back from her break yet. Soon she entered into the classroom, I lifted the letter to attire her attention.

Come out she said. She took the letter and said to me: Don't to be afraid just go tomorrow it will be ok.

Friday afternoon as the principal requested I went to see him in his office.

Have a seat my daughter. I called you because you run away from me before the school dismiss time for CHRISTMAS may I know the reason?

I first of all apologized to him for my behavior, and then I explained to him the all scenario of my engagement decided by my family. I explained to him the way that I felt about the situation and my opposition to be married to Vincent. I spent 30 minute crying without stopping. He looked me and said:

"Go my daughter it shall be well with you I will call my friend Gaston your uncle to talk to him".

I felt relief when he told me that. On my way to the classroom I saw Kadi seating at a secretary waiting for me. She wrapped me around her hams and asked me how it did go.

Everything is fine thanks Kadi I said to her.

Thank God he understood your concern. Now you can be relaxed at least one pressure is off of your shoulder she said.

It wonderful to have a friend who can really understand you Kadi was there for me when I needed it. She never turned me down instead she directs me and supports me in any decision that has taken. I will miss her a lot because she will not come back to school again. After her wedding, she is going to PARIS with her husband. I will never see her again unless by chance we meet during our life time. Now I will be left alone with my family, and I have to fund my way to continue my fight. I know that her husband will not allow her to write to any of her friend when she arrived to PARIS.

Three months later it was a summer vacation. This time my uncle did not send any letter to the principal of the school. He just wrote to me to ask me where I will spend my vacation. That he would like to see me in family during the summer vacation. I wrote him back and told him that I don't know if I will come or not, but I will think about it.

For the rest of the school time before summer I wrote to Francois to let him know that I will come soon the school is closed.

He replied back to me saying that he agreed that I can come, and he will send some money two weeks ahead.

The money that François sent to me came two weeks a head as he had promised. Five days later I took the money and when to buy my ticket for my trip. We only have six days left for summer vacation, but soon the final exam is over I will park my stuff to live.

Every year the school organizes a graduation party before we dismiss. But my friend Kadi and I will stay for the party. It was hard for Kadi and me to be separate forever. We have to fund a way to get in touch no matter what. I give to Kadi Francois's address so she can write me one day, but she said is not going to do it because of her husband.

I was counting the days left to go for my vacation. On Thursday which was the fourth and the last day of the final exam I put all my suite cases on my bed and share Kadi's bed that night.

Early in a morning on Friday, I put all my stuff out of the dormitory to wait for the taxis driver.

It was 7am when the first taxis driver pull over the dormitory.

All the cab drivers know that when the college is about to close for the summer vacation, every student will need a ride to go to town because the school is very far from the city, and nobody will be able to walk with his suite case in his hands, or on his head.

It was the moment that cab drivers also make a little bit of money.

Some of them got up early in a morning to be able to do more than three or five trip before noon.

One thing is sure I already have a cab and I will pay all the four seats to go to the train station as soon as possible in order to be on time for my trip to DAOUKRO.

All that I had in my head was my departure and my arrival to see Francois before night fall.

While the driver was approaching the bus station, I saw my legal guardian who was coming from his office.

My legal guardian was my cousin from my mom side. He was the CEO of the POST and TELECOMMUNICATION Company of the north department (KATIOLA).

I love him very much because he understand me and did not put any pressure on me even though everybody in a family was against my opinion of refusal to be Vincent's wife.

I used to call him Uncle Raymond. He was a handsome man with big eye very tall and love by women. He was a married man with two beautiful kids.

Soon I saw him coming from his office, I told the driver to go toward him.

When the cab pulls in front of him, I got out greeting him and saying goodbye.

He was furious and I know why because I did not tell him in advance that I was living the same day that the final exam was over. I understood his anger and I cannot blame him. I did not act right I apologized to him seriously on a bottom of my heart. He did accept my apologies and gave me some money after kissing me goodbye.

He paid the cab driver and gave him some extra money too. The driver was very happy and said thank to me as if I was the one who did give him that money.

The taxis arrived at the bus stop at 8am, but I still have one hour before my departure.

The driver helped me to collect all my stuff together before he leaves. I was very happy that I made it at the station one hour before, now I'm sure that I'm going for my vacation.

The wheather was nice summer time is always the best moment because it not cold like in DECEMBER.

The trip was very long, but it wasn't my first time to go to that city, so I field happier than concern.

I know that I will be there soon to be with François and that what matter to me.

After hours and hours of travel the bus finally arrived at destination around 5pmin the evening.

Francois was there to wait for me. He came to meet me while I was making my way to collect luggage.

Soon I saw him I forgot about what I was doing. I run like a five years old girl to jump at his neck and hug him.

I was much exacted to be with him because he gives me the desire to be what I want to be and we were also in love.

For me and for François life without one another was not possible. We were deeply involved in a serious relationship. We considered ourselves as husband and wife. There was not a doubt in our mind for sure. After few talk, we took a cab to go home. On our way home he told me that he had something to tell me but I will know soon we get home.

Usually when François come to pick me up at the bus stop, we go straight to the house, but this time we stopped to one of our relative and his wife to greet them. When I asked him why we did not go home, he answered that he has to go back to work therefore he doesn't want me to be alone in a house, so I have to stay with a couple until he come to pick me up. I was not quiet convinced of what he was telling me because even if he has to work I always stay home by myself, so why this time he doesn't want me to be alone home. I was questioned myself and thinking about everything that I could.

The couple offered me one of their rooms and told me to take my bath and to be relaxed.

After taking my bath I went to sleep for few hours before François come to pick me up.

At 8pm François came to get me, but what surprised me was that he proposed to the couple to come with us. I still don't get what was going on until we get close to our house.

While we were approaching the house I heard music and a lot of noise. I thought it was our neighbor, but it wasn't him the music was at François's house.

You are having a party François? I asked.

That was a surprise party for you my darling. You passed your final exam at the end of the year, and the reward for your hard work is to throw that surprise party for you.

Oh my God what did you do to me? I said to him.

As I was approaching the gate everybody run to me and lift me up on their shoulders and carried me to the house singing my favor song which is wonderful world, beautiful people of JYMMY CLIFT.

All I did was cried of joy. I never experienced such of attention and love.

My childhood was a little bit rough after my adopted mom who was my dad's cousin passed away.

All that I went through as child was forgotten since I met François. He was like a father, a brother and a husband to me.

He loved me more than I live myself.

What would I give back for such wonderful man that God has placed in my life? He has taken away all my sorrow. The only think that I can do is to love him back with all my heart and be faithful to him.

We did not have a lot of money, but the love that we shared was more than a wealth.

We paid attention to one and other, care about one and other.

We were committed to one and other. We do everything with respect and love.

It was impossible for us to be put apart one from another even for one day.

That type of strong love is like a poison that takes over your entire body, and carries you to the grave.

If one day François comes to die before me I will be in denied and his absence can cause my death because I will not be able to deal with the situation.

Our life was a real pleasure too much fun we had. Every day was different front another.

I could imagine that one day all our hope will be over because of the tradition.

It was in evening François and I decided to pay visit to one of our friend.

That night our plan was to invite our friend and his wife to a club after movie

After we had our dinner, we got dress to be ready for our evening plan, but it will not happen as we planned.

While I was putting my shoes in a living room, I head the gate bell ringing.

François, François someone is ringing the gate bell did you want me to go? I asked him

No it night time babe you are a woman never go to the gate at night when I'm not home even if I'm here never do it he replied.

I go babe said François and you get ready it must be our friend and his wife. Maybe they don't want to wait for us too long that why they came to us, so we can hurry up he said.

He rushes to the gate to open.

Unfortunately it wasn't our friend and his wife, but my mom and her two brothers.

Uncle Emmanuel side by side with uncle Gaston and my mother were standing at a gate.

They were so irritated, so upset, so furious, so angry at that point they did not even said hello to François.

They passed nearby him as if the house belongs to them.

They ignored him as if he did something wrong to them.

Of course for them what François has done was more than killing one of my family members.

Despite of their misconduct toward François, he honors them politely.

He asked them to sit down, and offered them some water, and drunks as the tradition required.

François sat between uncle Gaston and my mom, and I was close to Uncle Emmanuel.

I could describe my anger and frustration that night. How wish to have a power in order to vanish and live them sitting in that room alone. I felt like I was dying, but François was looking at me he was controlling all my movement. He knew that I wasn't happy about their unexpected coming.

He looked in eyes and told me to come in a room. Full of tears I followed him in a bedroom.

We both hugged each other and cried as we have never done. He holds my cheeks and looked me saying that we have to be strong that no matter what will happen tonight we have to overcome the situation.

He said to me ok don't be mad, calm down and we will see what they are going to do. Now we can go back to the living room and ask them the reason of their visit.

Back to the living room François and I sat beside one and other face to my family.

As the tradition required François started the procedure of news.

Uncle Gaston you and your family welcome to our home.

May I ask the reason why you came to visit us unexpected?

Without any comment, uncle Gaston told François that they came to get me because I'm a married woman who runs away from her husband.

OK uncle Gaston I have heard you, but since you and family have travel all day long and you are tired, I would like that you get some rest than tomorrow morning we can talk about your visit.

Our night and plan of going out has failed because of my family's presence.

We cannot let them home by themselves and go where we planned to go. Also the reason of their visit was an attack to our relationship. Instead of bringing peace among us, they brought sadness and disappointment into our peaceful life.

What would have done to deserve such of horrible situation in my life? Why can't they leave me alone live the way that I wanted?

Why do they want me to give on everything for someone's pleasure? Why me Francois I kept asking myself.

I refused to talk to all them. Even though I have seen them so long I felt like rejected.

Their actual presence was a handicap to my relationship, so for me there is no need to communicate to anybody.

Don't ask too much question said François any how we will win because they don't know that you are pregnant. Once they come to know about your pregnancy everything will be over.

He continued you see babe let me tell you that we won't be alone to fight against your family. Tomorrow I will call my uncle Leonard and his wife Martine to come to our house so all of us we can settle the situation.

Our friend and his wife since they did not see us at the time that we were supposed to be in their house, they took a cab and came over to see if everything was fine with us.

Surprise the bad news was waiting at the door to welcome them.

They were under the chock and did not know what to do. To be on our side they gave us some advises and promised us to be back at night fall for to meet my family together with Francois's uncle and his wife.

Francois and I let them to the gate and came back to the house to sleep.

That night was for me the longest night I had never had in my entire life. I could neither close my eyes, nor have a peace of mind until the sun rises.

Early in a morning I woke up to prepare their breakfast and after greeting everybody I set the table for them to eat.

They refuse the breakfast telling me that they didn't come to eat, but they came to take me to Vincent who is my husband to be. Francois is not going to be my husband even if I love him, or if we love each other that our problem all the want is to go with them if I want my family's unity.

My mom kept talking saying that if anything happened to her she will never forgive me for being disrespectful to her.

She continued saying that she has been humiliated in a family because of me.

What has she done to deserve that type of gift from me? I struggled to raise you and your brother up after your father and her cousin Felicity who adopted you passed way, and that how you will pay me back for all I did for you.

I replied to her that I did not do anything wrong to her, that all I did was to love someone and be love by that person in return. I did not kill anybody in a family it just because they don't want me to marry the person that I have chosen that all.

Mom I said to her. I know as you yourself know that I love you, and I will never do anything to disrespect you. I can even said that because I give you too much respect reason why you have that chance to force me to marry someone that I did not love.

Mom I did not do any wrong to you GOD knows if I did. One thing sure is that I wrote to Vincent himself telling him that I will never be his dream wife. He should have put this on his head and tell you all not to come here and disturb my peace with Francois. All that I have to say is to pack you stuff and leave the city tomorrow because I will not come with any one that is my final decision take it or not I will not give up to Francois don't waste your time and your money traveling to look for me.

Really are you sure of what you saying, and did you know the consequences of your action? Said Mom

I replied telling her that I know what I'm talking about and I will be ready to face any charge against me in any circumstances. I'm ready to face any tribulation to save my love for Francois. I will not accept any

Trough out the day my Mom and I spent our time discussing my marriage issue, and she noticed that nothing could change my mind. She turned to me with a sever look and said: <I can imagine how grown you have become at that point you can even take my advices any more>.

Mon I'm no longer a little girl who can do anything you want her to do. Time has changed and people also must change because we go to school to learn the best for our future not the worst for tomorrow.

She said: <Do you think that your school can teach you everything about social life than your tradition does? You nowadays generation you are so ungrateful all things. You take for granted our struggle to raise you up. Your only way to thank us as good parents for our well doing is to disrespect us. But I don't blame you I should blame the white man who allow women to go to school and forget about their place in the tradition society. I wished you never set your foot into the white man's school today we wouldn't be sitting here talking to you.

Sorry Mom, but I can't help it I replied.

Any way you know what to do my daughter because you are not going to be Francois's wife no matter what you. The does battle is not over and if you don't want to lose your life you better give up as soon as possible she said.

She had her mind fixed I had also made my decision and we will see who is going to win.

I told her that I was already pregnant for three months that they have to leave us alone it done it done nothing else can change the situation. She thought that I was kidding. For her it was a jock. It not possible that I could be pregnant that is a big shame for the family I can even died for doing that.

Oh yes Mom I'm three months pregnant. It not a lies mom I just don't want any of you to know that all.

Oh my daughter you have killed me. You see what you have done to your family? Hey God what did I do wrong to be humiliated that way?

As I confirm my maternity she collapsed and covered her face with both hand saying to me that I was curse to her. She said that I was very mean to do this to her as a daughter.

The entire day we did not talk about anything good but my marriage. Tonight again both family will come together to talk about the same matter what a shame.

My Mom my uncles refused to eat the food that I cooked for them.

When François came home, he found out that he food still on a table since lunch time. I told him that nobody want to eat our food because we are enemies of their progress.

That is ok said François let them be if they don't want to eat we cannot force. Don't argue with your mom to make thing worst that all I can tell you. Tonight everything will be over and we will have peace of mind.

At 6pm our couple friends and François's uncle with his wife came to the house to sit with my family and discuss about the issue of taking me back with them.

Soon uncle Gaston started he said to everybody this with a very calm voice: <I Gaston did not come here to talk about anything with anybody as far it concern I want my daughter to come with me that all I know not less not more that my rule and principal>

It takes more than four hours to solve the problem, but no solution was fund neither from my family nor from François's family. I refused to go and my family did not want to go without me.

Instead of spending one night with us my family stays over for four days. They sued François to the Governor of the county. The next day the appointment was fixed and we all have to meet to the counselors' office for my case.

François and I told the governor that I was pregnant, so there was no need to talk about anything else.

The chapter should be closed for good and never thank about it.

For my family even though they said yes to the governor because of my maternity, the battle was not over yet. Pregnant or not I have to be married to Vincent at any cost. He was the one chosen for me not François.

They did swallow their pride that day and came home with us. Soon we got home, my Mom parked everything that they brought included my own cloth and some of my item. According to her it just a first step of our battle, but it not over yet we don't need to celebrate until we hear from her.

They did not want anybody to give them a ride to the bus station; they took a cab and left the house as quicker as possible.

My mom before she left the house she said this to me: you better watch out because I'm coming back as soon as I can and more equipped than ever. And for your information, like it or not you have no choice. All you have to do is to follow my commands.

For my mom to said this words means that she will do what so ever she can to take me out there.

She will go to the native doctor to put a spell on me in order to obey them.

François and I have to be prepared for that situation. I know my mom she will do her best to get what she wants.

Since my family left us as time goes by François and I always think about the solution of our problem because we know that they will come back as they did plan, but we still don't know what type of strategy they will used to get us, we shall be ready to fight not for the last time, but to win for good.

My pregnancy was almost three months. Contrary to every woman during the first pregnancy I wasn't sick. I was doing pretty fine that make everybody believe that I wasn't pregnant. That the reason why my mom thought that I was laying to her about my being pregnant.

It has been two months since my family left us, and we don't know yet the time they will be back.

They are not going to tell us when they are coming one thing sure one day we wake up and see them at our gate as they did for the first time. We must be really prepared before their second arrival.

The only solution François and I had was to visit the native doctor for direction.

We want to know if we do anything to stop their action of putting us apart.

Any sacrifices that the situation required we will be ready to do it just to have our live back as it was.

In Africa back of those days, the native doctors were the only person who can determine whether or not the situation in which you are or your health condition will be better or not.

It wasn't a jock they have the ability to define your predicament or to predict what will happen to you.

It was really amazing sometimes I don't get it even though my mom many times did visit some of them with me, but I'm always surprise from one native doctor to another.

For the same problem my mom will go to more than two native doctors, and she will get the same answer before she stops. When I ask her mom why you always have to see more than two native doctors before you do what you want to do? Her answer is that I want to get the truth nothing but the truth before I do what I have to do. Based on my mother's way of doing thing and the type of talking she had with me before she left François's house I knew that she will go somewhere to fund her own solution to our separation. To be on the safe side I told Francois even though he had never gone to the native doctor I told him that we have to go and inquired about our union before my family take over the situation. He replied that for the sick of our love he will do it.

In a morning before he left for work, he let me know that he will talk to one of the employee that he trusts to see if he can get some help from him.

All day long I was home alone in a kitchen with my cheeks between my both hand thinking about Francois and I, how are we going to do what about if we get separate is possible that my family can do such of thing just to ruin our happiness for somebody else? I just can't stop torturing my mind over and over again. Around 1pm François came home from work while I was sitting in a shower room. I did not hear the door open because I was crying so loud and the water was running. I could stop crying it seemed like he heard me all the way to the living room. He suddenly opens the shower curtain and shot the water down. He clothed me with a towel hugged me and got me out of the tub. He made me sit at the hedge of the shower tub for few seconds and took me to the room to help me to get dress.

He can see that I was depressing as I never did in my life. I could even talk I just cried and cried over and over. He let me get some relieve then hold my hand and said to me to look him straight in his eyes.

As I look at him He said to me: <I will never ever let you go; unless death put us apart. Wipe your tears and be stronger than ever it will be fine. It just will be ok doing make me feel like I'm losing you. I spoke to one of the employee that I trust I did tell you right? He took me to the place this morning and you and me we are going there tomorrow I took off at work. Stop crying we will be ok>

Hearing these words I was a little bit relax, but I still thinking about the outcome of our visit to the native doctor tomorrow. What he is going to say my entire wish was a good result of what we wanted.

In the evening to make forget about the situation François proposed that we go to the movie and stop to our friends before we come back to the house. That decision did kick away my bad mood at least I can laugh for now.

For the rest of the day I was very happy but still I cannot get out of my mind the native doctor's visit tomorrow. I just cannot wait the day to come to see my family's failure in that battle between them and us. God knows what will be next only if he can give me a second eye to see in a spirit what will be our future, I would have be glad, but unfortunately I cannot see anything.

Saturday morning at 8am Francois told me that we have to go to the native doctor for our appointment.

Can he do something to save our love? Is he going to be able to help us?

We just don't know anything until we see him.

We have to leave now so we can come back quickly to the house.

The village where the native doctor lives was just 1hour away from the city.

It was a small village and everybody who lives there is related to the native doctor.

He had more than 2 wives the youngest one just gave birth to her first born.

The village was crowded of people who came to fund a solution to their problem.

We have to register in order to be seen by the native doctor.

We cannot rush until our turn comes to enter to the room.

After one hour of waiting, we finally were asked to enter into the room.

One thing that I did not like was the disclosure of the client's secret to all the visitors sitting outside on bench. Soon he saw François and me he shouted loud saying that I belong to someone else.

Revealing that to us, we did not even have courage to with him in a room, but we went anyhow.

In a room with the native doctor, he revealed that the battle between my family and us will be serious.

He told us that my family is not ready to give up; because their already know that we are not going to stay together.

We asked him if he can reveal the reason why we cannot stay together.

He replied that it is a very hard question to answer, that we have to consider the fact that we can't be husband and wife that all.

I knew that something bad will happen either to me or to François reason why he said that.

I guessed that he was afraid to tell us the truth in order to have a guilty conscience for the rest of his life.

I know one thing is that according the tradition the family members always inquire to know if the man their daughter have to marry will have long life or not.

But for this moment I had never thought about life or death before I get married to François.

It never comes to cross my mind that my family would have investigated to know if Francois will have a long life.

If they did, I may say because of my father premature death.

My mom was too young when my father died. My brother Paul at that time was 5 years old and I was less than a year.

That fear of being a widow after I have got married hunted my mother while I was growing up.

I remember telling me one day that she did not wants me to be married and be like her.

My mom was living in fear for my life. I understand that she should worry for me, but her transposition of being widow over my future I don't get it. She may be right or wrong I don't know.

The native doctor was précised telling us that we shouldn't try any other temptation of stay together.

He has spoken and came outside with us to say goodbye.

François and I were in tears because the native doctor said that there was no solution to our problem. We are not going to be married no matter what.

No discussion about our getting married. We asked ourselves why we cannot be married. What have we done so cruel to deserve that punishment?

Despite of the opposition of the native doctor and my family François and I did not give up.

For us that were a jock, we just can admit neither the truth, nor their predicament to our union.

We have our mind set up on something which was our staying together no matter what.

We decided to keep my pregnancy no matter what. We have made up our mind to keep our proms to one and other.

Our plan was to keep me to the city where François was working for the school year because of my pregnancy, so he can keep eyes on me since it was me first maternity.

Soon we came home, François told me that I should go back to my family to get every paper that I need for my transfer before the school start.

We were at two months of the school year beginning. I totally agreed with François that I have to go and get all my school document to come back.

Two weeks later I took a trip to go to my family, but I have to go to the village to see my grand mom and tell her goodbye.

I was very happy to go to the village because once in the village, I will also visit François's family, and everybody that I know.

Although I was happy to go to the village my fear kept increasing because of the people's judgment that I was about to face.

Nevertheless I kept my feelings stronger than ever, and I told myself that no matter what happen in a village I will not give up for sure.

It was Saturday morning the village market day when I arrived in a village. Uncle Edward wife Helen went to the village market with my grand mom, and they won't be back before 12 noon.

My mom will know that I came to the village even if I don't go to see her in my paternal village because people who took the same cab with me will tell her that I came. And I know soon she heard about my coming she will be in her village the very first morning to visit my Grand mom.

Before my pregnancy new spread all over the village, my mother will take me out of the village to send me to her half sister in the neighbor village just to cover me. I already knew what people will tell her about me, and she will not be able to be rude to them, because my mom always criticizes people's kids all the time telling that their parents did not teach them a good manor, but now it her own daughter who did not have a good manor what about that? What would she said? How would she defend herself about her daughter's <<prostitution>>?

Yes that is exactly the way the villages will put it. That I'm striper because I gave myself to someone who did not pay my bride price to my family and I'm pregnant of him. Good luck to my mother because she will face the all tribulation of everybody in a village.

I wasn't worried about neither my condition, nor what the villages will say to my mother. For me that am the beginning of the end of some cultures values that are applicable to every generation.

I was prepared while I was with my grandmother because I knew that my mom will come soon or later too take me somewhere in order to avoid the dishonorable situation that I put her in.

She doesn't get it. The solution is not to take me away from everybody, but to end the marriage against the young girls will.

As my grandmother were talking about are I was doing in her bedroom, I heard someone knocking at the door. Who is it asked grand mom?

Me Mahoua your daughter said my mother with a deep voice to express her unhappiness toward me.

Come in replied grand-mom. Oh I wasn't expected you today you told me at the market that you were coming tomorrow, so what made you change your mind all of sudden? Grand mom asked.

Well I thought the early the better that the reason why I change my mind.

What are you implying my daughter?

Nothing I just want her to visit her ante with me since she always as ked for her.

Well I think you should let her decide whether or not she really wants to go to see her aunt. Replied grand mom.

I really don't want to go nowhere grand mom it going to be some other time not this vacations. Is that ok with your mom? I said.

Fine do as you wanted, but me I'm telling you that tomorrow uncle Gaston and his wife Yolande are coming to get you for the city.

Why so quick mom? I just arrived to the village not more than 24 hours and we have to go to Abidjan tomorrow you guys are kidding me. That is a jock I said.

I'm serious my daughter and I mean every word that I said you are leaving tomorrow early in a morning with them.

Grand mom tell me that it not the truth what mom is saying to me. I don't want to go to Abidjan what about my vacations? And for what reason should I go with them to the city.

See my granddaughter it not matter of you, but it about the society that we are living in. Our environment count for us and our relationship with our neighbor matter the most.

As a grandmother who cherishes her granddaughter, I would like you to go with them to Abidjan.

Once again I busted into tears front of them. I have no choice I have to go with them, and once there I will figure out what I can do to escape from them and go back to Francois.

I did not even have a chance to visit Francois's family as I promised to him. I think that is not right, but who cares about my opinion for now. All that matter to everyone is to accomplish what they started.

Ok no drama I will go that is it. I want to avoid anything suspicious about my plan.

We left the village early in a morning as my mother said to go to Abidjan.

Next day after we arrived to Abidjan, aunt Yolande told me that we should see the Doctor as soon as possible because of my low stomach pain before the worst happen.

She said that the first pregnancy always gives some health problem, and to be on a safe side not just for me, but for the baby the Doctor has to see me.

Ok I was happy for that because for the first time since our litigation they are willing to help me to save my child. I will get relieve from the back pain and the low stomach pain.

I did not know what they were up to. I never heard about abortion in my life. I cannot even imagine that they can do it because my pregnancy was almost 4 months.

I wasn't aware of anything like that. Nobody ever mentioned something like that to me.

I was totally blind, and innocent of life experiences and its consequences.

At night fall ante Yolande told me not to eat anything not even water from midnight till we come back from the Doctor's appointment.

She told me that the type of physical that I have to do is very important, and if I dare eat the Doctor will not be able to see me that day.

I knew that I was in constant pain so I obey to her, and did what she told me to do.

Early in a morning aunt Yolande came to my room to tell me to get ready.

Aunt YOYO she was called. That was the nick name that we give to her.

She was such of beauty woman. She had a very light skin, and her skin lightness was different from any other light skin color. It seemed that both of her parents were Chinese, and she also looked like a Chinese women.

She was a very nice lady always available to do what she does for people in need.

She is always telling jokes to make you laugh.

She had never called me by my real mane, but by my nick name which is grand mom.

She was very sweet to me, and I can't replace her for the rest of my life. I will always miss her and she will always be in my memory for ever.

She married to my uncle without knowing him. She had never met my uncle before married him.

She was chosen by my grandfather while she was 1year old to be uncle Gaston's future wife.

She told me that people always tell her that she has a husband who is an administrator in a city.

She never asked her parent who he was, and from which village did he come from.

She was going to school and her father was the first general secretary of the fist political party of the country (PDCI-RDA) He was also an elementary school teacher in a city.

Her grandfather was one of the famous KINGS in the county who had more than 6 wives.

Despite all the riches of her family she got married to someone she had never met who was my mom's second brother.

Thank God for her she had a very happy marriage life. She was loved not only by my uncle, but also by the entire family.

To end her conversation with me, she told me that she wished me a good luck to be happy in my marriage as she was in hers.

I'm stepping out grand mom now you can get dress so we can be to the Doctor as soon as possible.

While I was getting myself ready, I was thinking about that entire she just told me about how she got married to my uncle. Why would she tell me her story? Did she want me to do like her or what?

I have no clue. I just need to harry up to get dress and leave the room before she comes back.

Soon I was ready I want to her and tell her that we can leave.

Ok good let go I will get in touch with your uncle when we finish.

She told one of the boys in the house to call the cab for us.

Few minutes later the driver came and pulls over the house entrance.

He can someone handle me my purse in the living room please.

I go get your purse ante. I run to the living room and brought it to her in a car.

Driver she said to him we are going to Doctor ACHY's CLINIC. Do you know the place or you want me to show you?

No Madamme I know where it is doing worry, we will be there before 9AM.

Ok thanks SR

You welcome Madamme.

Forty-five minutes later we reached the CLINIC.

One thing that I noticed in that clinic it that all the patients were young girl's. They all between 18 years old to 20. They were sitting in a lobby with their family members or with parents.

Soon my ante and I entered one of the employee came to us and told us to have a sit that the Doctor will be out soon to see me.

Why all the patients are less than 30 years old I ask my ante.

She replied telling me that the youngest are the one always in trouble that is the reason why they are here to see the Doctor.

We sat for about 40mn then the Doctor came out to see us.

MS BAH said the Doctor to my ante how are you doing this morning? I hope that you brought me a good new from my dear friend your husband.

Well I think so Doctor.

Come in with your niece. She will stay here to wait for the nurse who is going to prepare her then I will come later.

The nurse gave me a shot and the first thing that I noticed when I woke up was that I was no longer pregnant, but I was having some strong pain in my low stomach more than before.

I was bleeding and the rest of the day I was very sick than was before I came to see the Doctor.

What did he do to me? I asked my aunt, but she didn't answer to me.

Can you tell me at least what is going now here with me? Why all that bleeding comes from?

She just shook her head and told me not to be worried because it was over.

What I am over what are you talking about aunt? I felt like I have no more my baby aunt.

Why aunt why you guys did this to me, what would I tell François about everything that just happened.

Well that is the reason why I told you that you do not have to worry about anything.

Forget about François because he is no longer part of your life and you will not be part of his.

Just like that aunt? How can I forget about him in couple minutes?

I know that my life is going to be miserable from now and on. What my family just did to me is unforgettable, but I still will not give up yet on François.

Since I'm sick I will wait till I get better then I will escape to go to the city where François lives, and tell him everything that they did to me. I was supposed to stay with my family for about one month at least, but what they did to me change my mind.

Two weeks later, I escape from the house and went to François.

He wasn't expected me at that moment, but I had no choice, but anticipate my vacation.

I left the town at 5am in a morning before everybody gets up in a house. Nobody knows what my plan was because I did not discuss anything with anybody.

I took the first but whish was going to DAOUKRO the city where Francois lives. Around 2pm the bus arrived to the bus stop. I called the cab to drive me to Francois's job because I knew that at this time of the day he will be at work not at home. Few blocks later we arrived at the job place. I paid the driver and tell him to come back later on to drop me off home.

One of François friend was the first to see the driver pulling over, he run toward me and after exchanging few words he told me to wait that he will take me home because since two days Francois did not come to work. He was sick and took some days off.

I was very sad about it. How will I do to give him another brokenhearted new knowing that he has been sick for couple days now, and who know maybe he is thinking about all the situation that I may go through with my family. I really don't know where to start when I get home. That is going to be a painful moment that he had never had in his entire life because of my family.

About 3pm François's friend and I arrived to the gate of the house. I couldn't stop thinking how I have to tell François before night fall. I think I better keep quiet for few days until he gets better than from there I will know what to say.

Soon he saw me at a gate he run to me and picked me up. I was waiting for you to come. I thought that I'm sick because of your absence now that you are here I feel better I can say.

Ah François so you have a love sickness? You should have tell me I would have called your wife to come back as soon as possible said his friend.

Ok here is your wife I came to drop her I'm going back to the office let me know if you need anything from me my friend.

Thanks Justin I really appreciated that you rendered me that type of service, I owe you a big time.

I have to keep the secret for couple days till he goes back to work then I will have a courage to announce that bad news. It was Saturday night three days after I arrived to him that I decided to break the new.

Sitting in a living room I started talking about my return to school for the semester, and my family's plan for me to be with them.

As I was talking, he stopped me in a middle of my conversation and asked me this:

You did not tell me how things went with your family. How everybody is doing and how are they

Copping with your pregnancy?

I could hold myself to answer to his question, all that I did was crying over and over.

What make you cry? They treated you bad isn't it? Is that the reason why you came back so early? Then you don't have to worry because I'm glad that you came sooner than later.

No, François none of what you are thinking.

I just don't know where to start and how to tell you about what happen to our babe.

Our babe why? What are you talking Loren. What was wrong? What did they do to you?

I lost the babe? I'm sorry it wasn't me. They did it

You did an abortion? They took you to the Doctor to do it? Who did go with you? How can they hate me so bad at that point?

I'm going to kill your uncle and whosoever calls himself your husband.

I just can't deal with this anymore, it was my fault I wasn't supposed to send you to them I should have done it my babe would have been a life.

What I have done to your family to deserve that?

I'm sorry babe I really I'm

Forgive me. I wished I could have done something to help myself.

I did not know anything about abortion.

My aunt told me that we have to see the Doctor because of the low stomach pain that I was having.

We went and the time that I got up everything was done.

I'm sorry if I knew I would have gone with her.

That is ok it over we can do nothing about it now because the situation is irreversible. Stop crying and get over it I forgive you. You have to know one thing next time I will not send you to anybody for anything. You will stay here until you give birth if you get another pregnancy.

That chapter was over, but it was a painful one that I will never forget about all my entire life because something was taking out of me. François is a man he can forget about couple months even later in his life time, but I as a babe carrier I would not forget and forgive my family.

The second year of our relationship started already and I was pregnant again for the second time.

I was doing fine, and everything between Francois and I was pretty much good I can say.

W e decided not to visit my family again. I cut off every contact with them. They were living far away from where François and I live. It takes more than 16 hours to reach the city where François lives.

In my mind the trouble was over for good with my family. If I see them again my babe may be one year.

Our life was a peaceful one. I was still going to school without any problem.

My pregnancy was more than 3 months I was very happy about it.

My second pregnancy was kind of our last solution. It made me forget about the lost of my first babe.

All that I was thinking about was the time to deliver my babe. I know that for the second time my parents will be disappointed at me therefore they will give up on us. I thought that soon they come to know that I was having babe they will understand to give us a peace.

Somehow my heart was not in peace even though I tried to forget about the past pregnancy.

How I wish to give birth now before another problem occurred again with my family.

One night while we were with some of our friend in our house, we heard the door bell ringing.

François runs out to see who was at a gate. Soon I heard Francois screaming I knew that my family came back again to disturb us.

It was my family again for the second time I was totally right.

You came back again in my house? After all you have done.

You killed my babe and you have a nerve to come back here to my house?

What have we done to you to deserve this for Christ sake?

Why we can't live our life like everybody else?

I'm sorry, but I don't want you in my house that is it.

Go somewhere else to get help but I'm not going to take you in my house no way I can't allow you in my house for what you did to me and my wife.

I just can't believe it after one year you came back to torment us again.

I want you out of here before I kill one of you.

Get out of my house as soon as possible. I want you all to get out of my site before I open my eyes.

I can't just believe on my eyes that they really came back again. François was irritated he kept screaming get away from us go and don't come back here no more.

He was so loud that our entire neighborhood came out to see to whom he was talking to.

He was crying, so I also was why God? Why this time again? I can't take this anymore Francois said.

For about 2 hours they were standing there by the gate because he really did not want them to cross the gate. He was sitting at a gate holding his head with his both hands.

I rather died than let them in my house he said to one of our visitors.

No said one of our friends to him. François let them in. Don't allow any hanger to take over your mind now. Let it be if she is meant to be your wife she will be. Don't do anything stupid and you will end up regretting.

As his friend spoke to him, he let my family by the gate and came inside of the house without them.

Justin at that moment decided to calm down everyone and brought them in the house.

Our friend Justin and his wife were forced to stay with us for another couple hours. Before Justin left, he told François to think about what he had just told him. Don't do anything wrong till I come back tomorrow Justin said to François.

Justin told my family to come with him to his house to avoid any other situation during the night.

They went with him without saying anything to us. I was really amazed the way my mom was calm.

That type of attitude of my mom was very suspicious to me. I really don't know what they are planning against us.

I was right about my mom's being cool attitude. Of course I know my mom. When she acts peacefully that means she has something in her mind that he wants to accomplish. She is taking chances to get the best result and be happy about her action.

She was carrying a peanut with the skin in her purse. That peanut was prepared by one of my cousin Flan's native Doctor for my break up with Francois in a short period of hours.

Uncle Flan's native doctor was from BENIN the country where all kind of woodour power was common.

That native doctor put a spell on a peanut with shells to give it to my family for me.

He told them that if I eat the peanut I will forget about Francois. I will never feel I same way I felt for him before.

She knew that I love peanut and the only way to get me is to us the peanut. One thing sure I will eat that peanut without problem. The native Doctor told her to just put the peanut on a table while she is talking to me at a same time. I will eat and as far as I'm eating it my mind will change toward François.

He told her that before the peanut finish, I will think about my family and I will take my decision to go with them, but they don't have to fight with us otherwise it is not going to work, and I will stay with him and become a widow after couple years of marriage because Francois doesn't have long life to live.

If I may understand there was only one reason why my family did not want me to get married to Francois. He doesn't have long life to live. So that was the reason why the first native Doctor that Francois and I went to see said that we are not husband and wife. He said that we are not going to stay together no matter what we do.

He was right for that. Those supernatural forces you can't go beyond them, and you can't understand how they work, but you get to believe it they are real.

My family stays with Justin for two days before they came back to our house. That night when my family came back to the house they were very polite to François and presented to him their excuses for what they had done to me in a past regarding our first babe.

We all were sitting around the kitchen table. Suddenly my mom put out from her purse a small bag of peanut with a skin. She just did as the native Doctor instructed her.

I was the first one to put my hand in a bag and started eating one by one. We were all eating, but since it was charmed on my name I'm the one targeting.

We ate and talk about my childhood and some other staff about Francois and I when we are going to see them so they marry us traditionally.

One hour after eating the peanut, I started thinking about the way my mom did struggle to raise us after my father past away.

My thought was completely guide by my conscience which I did not have before their second return to our house.

All that I was thinking was to follow my parents no matter what. I can't abandon my family because of man I started thinking about all this.

My brain was totally washed and renew. I don't worry any more about François and me. All that matter to me was my family I have to go with them that all I know. Francois was out of my mind for now.

I had no control over what I was doing or thinking about. It was unbelievable that I changed all of sudden.

François was in a room while I was talking to my mom and Uncle Emmanuel about my decision to go with them at last. I mean it and I will do it mom because I really want to go with you. My family comes first the rest is after. I can see my mom's face while I was talking to her. She felt a relieve, and that was her goal, but I was taking that decision without my own conscience it wasn't me talking, but the spell put on me was doing what it was supposed to do.

Soon I finished talking to my mother, I run into the bedroom to call François.

What is it? What did your mom told you to do? I hope you are not changing your mind isn't it?

I know François the decision is not easy for me. See if I denied my family tomorrow and something did happen to us I will be a shame to face them.

Please trying to understand me let me go with my family I will be back I proms.

He was very angry about my decision. He did not want to hear anything about my living.

What about our baby have thought one second? What about me? Now you are taking your family's side and here I'm by myself. I look like a foul to them because you are not with me anymore.

Why you doing this to me can't you see that I need you more than ever?

I let everything because of you. I gave up to my school to work and make you feel comfortable.

Now that I need you, now that I can have hope of our future here we are, it all over for good.

Don't do this please don't go no matter how we will overcome the situation.

I want you to stay until you give birth then you can leave please don't say no to me babe.

Tell your mom that you will come later. You cannot just leave like that. Think about us we come from far to let everything go just like that.

He kept begging me over and over again.

He was crying like a two years old boy whose mom was leaving him.

I busted into tears and kneed down to grasp his feet and can't stop crying.

I really don't know what to do François looks my mom she is so sad and worried about me.

Let me go tomorrow with them if it God's will that I belong to you, I will be back to you.

He replied to me saying that how would I know that it is God's will or not? That I had never spoke like that before. Why all of sudden I became totally different, and I see him as a stranger to me. What have they done to you babe tell me I don't recognize you anymore. It seems like you have never met me before. God what is going now here we need some answers from you.

Are you really going tomorrow with your family? Is it true what you are telling me?

I just can' believe on my own eyes. No that is not you talking something must be wrong somewhere I'm sure of that.

We couldn't sleep during the night François was so worried that he wished that the night will never be over.

He said to me: <I know this is our last night together something is telling me that I will never see you again even that pregnancy I doubt that it will stay. I just want you to know one thing that I love you no matter where you will be, and if it happen that one day I may died before I go, I will send you a message to come and see me before I leave this world>.

Early in a morning, François went to call Uncle Leonard and his wife Martine to come and talk to my family in order for them to leave without me.

Uncle Gaston told him that they did not ask me to go with me I'm the one who took the decision to go with them. They knew what they are done to me, the spell that my family put on me was irreversible. I have no longer a full control of my own thought. I was present physically, but my mind did not belong to me anymore. I had no regret of what I was doing to François neither to myself. M y conscience was totally absent. I did not belong to myself as I was before the spell. All that I know is to leave the house as soon as possible. Get away from him that is it.

The next day we did not leave the city. My family has to stay for another night because François had called some of his friends to intervene for him, so I won't leave hum. It was too late my mind was processed by the spell, and nothing did work out. The third day early in a morning we left the house for the bus station.

I knew how painful it was for François to stay in that house without me, but I can' realize anything for that moment. It wasn't me at all every though of mine was dictated by the black magic power.

All that I have to do was obeyed to the command of the evil spirit in me.

As we traveling my mom asked me if I really want to go with them.

Yes mother I want to go with you and stop worrying yourself it over I promise.

Are you sure my daughter that you are not coming back to François?

No mom I will not come back to him I will get marry to Vincent if that makes you happy.

Thanks my daughter I knew that you will not disappointed me because you never done it.

One year later, I was sent to Vincent brother in Gagnon for my schooling while he was at his last year of law faculty in Abidjan. The following year, Vincent won the national scholarship for the law school in Paris. He has to leave the country for two years before he comes back, and I have to stay with his family until he comes.

During those two years that he spent in Paris I have to remain faithful to him. Every move that I made was under control. I have to defend my family's honor and Vincent's.

Something that really amazed me was that Vincent had a girl Friend who always come to visit his family, but he had never told her who I was to him. I remembered when he was student at campus she used to come around every weekend and whenever she comes, he will tell his brother Alex to take me home to his family. Since I never shown any sign of jealousy toward her she always thought that I was Alex's girl friend.

Any letter that Vincent sent to her from Paris she will come and show it to me, and I was surprised that the same thing that he wrote to her was the same that he wrote to me too. If he sent me a picture he will send the same picture to her. For her we are sisters in law our husband is brothers, so we should be good friends. I play my role of smart young lady, and pay attention not to reveal to her who I really was to Vincent. I kept the secret and nobody in Vincent's family will volunteer to tell her what is going on.

Those two years, Vincent's girl friend and I were so closed that sometime she asked me some advises. One time she revealed to me that Vincent was the first and he will be the last man of her life. That when he comes back from Paris they will get married, and she would like me to be there because when Alex comes back from Paris she will be there for me.

Poor girl I felt so bad for her I wish I can tell her who I really was, but I can't she is not going to believe me. She has been waiting for Vincent all her life now looks what is happening to her oh God.

We all waited two years or Vincent to come, but during his training in Paris he felt in love with another lady. She also won the national law school scholarship for Paris, and they decided to get married when they come back from Paris.

None of his family was award of the situation. He had made up his mind to move to her place soon they come back from Paris, so they both can stay together as a couple.

Two weeks after Vincent came back from Paris, he told me that he was going to his girl friend's house.

He said to me: here I will leave this money, you can buy anything you want, and you can come and see me if you need me. If that money is not enough, come to see me I will give you more>.

I wished he would have said to me that he was sorry for it happening, and for what he did put me through. I wish he would have asked me to forgive him.

He had no remorse of what he did. Everything was normal to him. Thing should be in that way because he was the one who controlled the situation nobody else. That is the power of abuse of a reach young man like him. The only person who asked to forgive Vincent for what he has done to me for those two years was his cousin Lambert and his wife were a stay during my school vacations.

Yes forgive Vincent after two years of waiting on him. I t so easy to say it. I wished he would have never set his eyes on me before; today I would have been humiliated in that way.

Soon his cousin spoke to me, I run in a house and stood front of Vincent to release all my anger.

You are so selfish so rude so brutal, so unpredictable I don't even know how to qualify you and which word I should used to descript your character.

All that I went through with my family because of your money, all that François went through you and your money, and my family I will hate all of you for the rest of my life. I wished you go to hell for ever.

You can never replace what have been taking from me. Your selfish desire and womanizer sicknesses will send you to fire when you died.

I think you need some help from God to set you free from your psychological behavior.

How many victims you have left, and who is going to be your next target.

I hope that God forgive you and good luck to you for your life.

After few days of reflection, I made up my mind. I realized that he doesn't deserve me why would have hold on to something which is not mine. I can't fix what has been done my past will always be in my mind as a hurt feeling. I will never forgive myself for the second abortion that I volunteer to do just to obey to my family's desire of marrying Vincent. Deep in me the wound will remain without cure for the rest of my entire life I will live in a guilty conscience.

I already lost two pregnancies, and I can't go back to Francois not because he not going to take me back, but I did not have any feeling for him due to the spell my family put on in order to put me away from him. What a disaster for my life, at age 19 my love trial already started.

I told him that it was ok with me, but the only thing that I would like him to do, was to call all my family and his family and together they can set me free, so I can go anywhere I want to go, and I can marry any one that I want.

H e refused to do it, and his family wasn't happy about what he was about to do. They all told him to release me. He has to let everybody know that he was no longer interesting in me.

I cannot just sit there for him while he will be living with someone else.

When the government sent him to one the city in a Central of the country called BOUAKE I have to move there with him. With his family's pressure, he gave up on the woman that his was to marry.

Once we arrived in BOUAKE he felt free to do whatsoever he wanted to do. We were left by ourselves now. Nobody will pay attention to what he is doing. He some started dating women of my age, some of them older than me. One of them was his legal mistress, and she was allowed to share the bed with me whenever I'm not around. Even if I came for vacation and she is already in the house with him, I will sleep in the other room and let them be. I was like a second hand to him.

I don't need to go to school because that what he wanted. I have to put back all those school years and be home as a decoration frame in a house. I was home with a maid who does everything all I do was to eat and be my own boss, but that was not the type of life that I wanted. I want to finish my school and be someone one day. I don't want to depend on a man, and all those years that I did at school I'm not going to waist them for him.

In that city where we were living, he was a Judge of the tribunal or First Instance. A man highly respected at work, but at home he was another person, and I think that he needs a counselor himself.

I could take it any more from him. He goes anywhere I wanted to go with his girl friend while I was there in a house. Sometime his new girl friend will come home just to show her to me. Just to let me know that I was in that house for a price.

I told myself that I'm only 20 years old, and I still have a lot of thing ahead of me, so why should I make myself miserable for someone who doesn't appreciate what he has.

I told myself that I have no more time to waist. I have to do something to get out from his house.

I took my decision not to share the same bedroom with him. I want to respect myself if Vincent doesn't respect me. I told him that I will never sleep in a same room with him anymore, so I transfer all my stuff to the other room.

We were in a separate bedroom for 6 months, and I never shown anybody that something was going on between us. I kept everything cool to figure out what I can do to set myself free indeed.

Every weekend he goes to another girl friend in another city, and leaving behind him some money for me just in case I need it.

I called my uncle and let him know how thing where going in my house, but he told me that I should not back up.

He doesn't want to hear anything about my going back to them.

For more than three weeks I thought about my plan, and I came up with the solution.

I wrote to one of my college classmate also call Vincent. I begged him to do me a favor to write me a letter as if I was his girl friend and send it to the house address.

One week later, I received that letter, and intentionally I left it on top of the bedroom dresser where he can see it.

When Vincent saw the letter, he called right away my ante and my uncle to come. He told them that we have an emergency situation going on. At that moment I knew that I will be set free soon.

In my tradition if the woman commits an adultery she is subject of humiliation therefore she is not supposed to stay with her husband. He has to divorce her immediately. She will go back to her family, and they have to reimburse the bride price no matter how.

I was ready to leave soon they my family comes. I was prepared for the consequences of my action.

All that I wanted was to go far away from him and never set my eyes on him again.

Unfortunately hen they had the reunion, he decided that I should stay. He didn't want me to leave.

Why would he accept me after all that I did? He just wanted to punish me that all I can say otherwise why not let me go.

I couldn't do anything and I can't decide to leave since he didn't tell me to go, but I don't want to be in his house for another year. What else can I do?

Three weeks after my family left Vincent was getting worst. Every weekend he was gone and will come back Monday after work. I was in a house as an object of decoration. If I can say it I was a collage in that house. His girl friend will come and go as she wanted. The one that knew before his departure to Paris for his Law School training also came one time to visit us. That night I allow him to share the bed with her and I will stay in the other bedroom. I did it because I know how she feels. I did not want to fight neither with him nor with Anne. I mean traveling about 6thousands kilometers to come and see him, and discover that I, the one she used to share everything with about Vincent was there with him?

How many time she shown me the letter and pictures that Vincent used to send to her.

She trusted me and I never told her anything about my relationship with Vincent.

I kept it secret until she herself comes to know it now. I owe her for what I did to her, so I let her have the room, so she can forgive me. One month later after she was gone we got a new that she was pregnant from Vincent.

Everybody was blaming me for allowing such of thing to be happening.

I did not make I mistake doing this contrary of what people may think, I was happy of my action. I felt relieve somehow in my mind. I know Vincent will not marry her, so she is not a winner as she thought she was. None of us even his new girl friend he will not marry her.

One night we had a visitor. It was one young lady names Fatou and her mother. Vincent introduced to them to me as our niece because her mom was from our side, but married to a Mulsuman from the North. I could have never known that Vincent will marry that woman that he introduced me as our niece. For the moment that he brought her home I knew that she was his new girl friend in a town.

Now he has more than three girl's friend in a city and one out of city.

Should I continue to humiliate myself because of my family's blindness or their stupid thinking of having a lawyer as a son in law? Non I have to find my way out this time without their consent.

I wrote to my uncle and told him that from the time that he will received my note I will no longer living in Vincent's house. What I had in my mind as a final decision was to kill myself for them and that it is.

That month of February 1984 there was a series of movie called DONNA BENJA. The movie was from Argentina and every Wednesday before 6pm everybody sat front of their TV to watch it. The next movie after DONNA BINJA was DALLAS of Bobby and Sue Ellen.

Wednesday night was pretty much a busy night for the all town. The streets are almost empty because everybody is home watching those two movies series.

While everybody was concentrated on a movie I went in a room and took 31 tablets of valium. After taking them, I came back to the living room as nothing wrong with me. Later on I left the house for no way. I was walking on a street for an unknown direction. I just want to died that all.

How it is going to be I don't worry about it. I just wanted to be set free once for good that is it.

The last thing that I remembered when I was falling was a strange voice saying to me no. The sound was so loud in my hears and repeatedly until I lost conscience. The next day I found myself in BOUAKE CENTER HOSPITAL bed after the gastro intestinal cleaning. I didn't have any ID with me to identify me.

I was very tired, weak, my stomach was hurting me and I was very sleepy. I ask the Nurse in charge if she have seen the person who brought me here.

She said to me: <My daughter thank God that you are alive today. They found you in a pit and they called the fire work department to take care of you. The time that you got here it was only 30mn left for you to be no longer in this life. The person who found you refused to reveal his identity, but he told us that you will survive anyhow. He came here to the Hospital with the fire department then left after we gave you a room. I personally told him to wait until you get up, but he refused. He stood for 20 second looking staring at you wiping his tears than left after blessing

me and telling me to take care of you. All that I can say is that the angel of the mighty God has brought you here by himself>.

As the Nurse was talking to me the Doctor knocked at the door.

Come in said the Nurse. He introduced himself telling me what happen if need anything and who are my parents how they can get untouched with them. I can give Vincent's name because he is a judge at the tribunal of instance. Everybody knows him I don't want him to lose his job, so I gave his uncle's name.

The Doctor kept asking me if I had a problem with my family or with my husband. What made me do such of thing to myself? Life is so precious to take it away. God gave you life He is the one who should take it back. Don't offer yourself to leave the world because you did not bring yourself into this world my daughter. Next time think twice before you do another stupid thing because once you are gone you are gone. And whatsoever problem you are running away from killing yourself is not the solution as you think. Do you understand clearly I'm saying this for your good?

Yes Doctor I answered I will never ever do it again. Thanks for saving my life I really owe all of you.

Before he left the room, he told the Nurse to check my blood pressure and withdraw some blood for the lab to see the level of the drug that I took in my system.

Nurse I said to her. Thank you for telling me everything about my coming here last night.

You welcome my daughter just is careful sometimes. You should have someone to talk to avoid all this.

I volunteer to tell her everything that was going on in my life.

Oh God you see it seems like I knew it she said. You should be open and trust someone who can carry your burden on his shoulder. A friend to whom you can tell all your struggles. You see my daughter life is like a soccer field every player would like to score and be the lead of the team, but sometimes they forget the adversary front of them. He will also try to protect his team. Your adversary will fight to win, so you have to resist if you want to be a winner of the game and have your trophies. That life we have to fight stand firm trusting ourselves, so we can be a winner.

You should never try to kill yourself again, never ever you heard me.

Yes Nurse thanks for your advises I will always carry them in my heart to remember you.

One week later I was discharge from the Hospital. Vincent came to get me with his driver.

I can't wait to go home and park my tuff for my journeys. I want to go to my brother and see what I can do. I spent the whole night thinking about what I will do when I get out from Vincent's house.

Early in a morning before he left for work. He gave me some money and told me that I can go to his brother house in Gagnoa for few weeks. I did agree and left the next day.

Soon I get there, I told his brother that I want to go to the neighbor country to retake my GED.

Have you talk to Vincent while you were coming to me?

No I replied, but I have to go because I don't want to stay home this year without doing anything.

Ok you will, but let me try to explain to Vincent what you want to do. I know that he will talk to him. The spoke to Vincent about my going to BURKINA FASSO. I think he told him not to let me go, but uncle Anatole did not agree with Vincent. He insisted in order for me to go for my school before it too late. Vincent told him that if I crossed the line of the city where I was with his brother, than I rather consider myself as a single woman.

Vincent brother was working at the electricity company in GAGNOA. Amatole he was called, his wife's name was Rose they are sweet and nice people. They always take me as their own daughter. They love me so much at that point they fight sometimes with Vincent on my behalf. I remembered when I was in a high school in Gagnoa.

One night I had crises of appendix at the boarding school, and the school had to take me to the Hospital urgently. That time the city was having a problem of electricity because they were doing some work to intensify the level of the electricity in a town. For that reason, the squares had to take a turn to have a light. Every two hours another square will have a light and another two hours it will be another square turn.

That night, Vincent's brother told my school principle; to go to the clinic instead of the hospital.

He told them that he was on his way to meet them to CLINIC LE FROMAGER of Doctor KEITA one of the famous Doctor in the city and in the country also.

The square where the CLINIC was had one hour of electricity left before they switch to another square.

Soon we entered to the CLINIC the nurses took me right away to the surgery room.

The clinic has an electricity group for the emergency situation like mine, but my brother in law Amatole called his boss, and told him that he had his daughter in a surgery room therefore he is asking them to prolong the electricity hours in the square were the clinic was located until they finish my surgery.

Considered that that it done I will give an order the worker to extend the hours for your daughter's emergency situation.

I was very lucky that day and I never forget that night also. I will be always grateful to Amatole and his wife Rose for showing me such of big love.

Uncle Amatole as I used to call him had paid all my one week clinical bills and the fees of the surgery.

He took me home instead of the boarding school, and I stay with them for one week before I go back to the boarding school.

Such of love I will never forget about it.

At night fall he came to me in living room where I was watching a TV. There were three of his daughters, Chimen, Felicite, and Noelle. He told me that he will give me the transport when he comes back from work tomorrow.

The next day he did as he said. He gave me the money and told me to take care of myself.

I gather all my cloth and whatever I may need for the journey.

Honestly speaking, I was very happy to go. I felt such a relieve in my spirit to be set free at last.

I went to Abidjan where I was supposed to take the train for BURKINA FASSO the next day.

Three day later I want to BURKINA FASSO. The city where I stay was Bobo Dioulasso. My school was in Banfora one of the rich town of BURKINA FASSO. LYCEE MODERN ET CLASSIC DE Banfora was the school that I was supposed to attend that year.

I had a very nice scholar year in that city. I had a lot of friend and we all study together.

After my exam on JUNE I came back to Vincent's place to collect my cloths, but my surprise was big.

He torn all of my cloth and put them back to the suite case. When I arrived to his house, he refused to give them back to me because I told him that I was coming to get them. He thought that I was coming to stay. I told him that I have to leave and I did not come to spend the night to his house.

So you came to get you cloth. Try me I will kill you before you leave this place he said.

Killing me you said? not in this house I will not died in your house, and you will not do anything to me until I leave your house I replied.

We started fighting physically and he was so furious as if I took anything from him.

It over Vincent I will not turn back never ever again. Forget about me anyway I have never been part of your life o what is the deal let me go I don't have nothing to do with you again. You don't want to give me those cloth, fine you can have them as a souvenir from me.

He was chasing me everywhere in the house. He grasped a mortar wood in a kitchen to knock me down to death, but one of his nephews who saw him yield saying to me to run away.

I will kill you and nobody will say anything to me he added.

I jumped over the fence of the yard to fall on the other side of the wall.

I quickly called the cab to take me to the bus stop.

The bus was about to leave when the cab pull over. I took my ticket and went to have a sit. While the bus was getting ready to leave, I saw Vincent's car through the window.

I quickly bow my head because Vincent can tell the bus driver to pull over if he saw me in.

That the abuse of the power when people have money they can touch the sky.

Thank God he did not see me. Now I can roll the stone and throw it at my back because the chapter has been closed forever and ever. No more Vincent in my life no more my family on my back.

It was the beginning of a new life for me. I don't know for what reason he has to write to me. What was he thinking about? Did he think one second about what he done to me? I don't think that he has a conscience of what he did otherwise he would have wrote me a letter.

At my first university year, he wrote me a letter saying that he was sorry for what he did. He wanted me to go back to him.

I did not reply to his letter I just took it and handle it to my family. I told them that I don't want to hear anything from him for the rest of my life.

Since then it has been more than twenty years that I have seen Vincent, or hear from him.

Twelve years later I dreamed about François. In my dream he came to me and tells me that he was about to travel, but it going to be a long journey. He showed me the place where he was going. It was a very deep place down the hill, and so slippery all the house at that place were very strange. I asked him how he can leave his family to go for a long journey. And how can he go to a place so deep like that one with a motor cycle. He answered to me that his time has come to travel. He said to me that I should care about Gertrude his first daughter who has his ex girl friend's name.

One thing was that when Francois was I life, he loved motor cycle a lot. Sometimes he rides with me to go to another square just for fun.

That night that dreamed about him, early in a morning, his niece that I had seen for almost 10 years come over to my brother's house. I was sleeping when my mom called me, and notified me that she was in a living room.

I had seen her for about 10 years since the day that I left Francois's house. How comes she came over to see me. Soon I heard her voice I run into the living room.

What brought you here so early? Is everything ok with François? I had a dreamed about him this morning around 5am I said. Don't tell me that something happen to him. I just don't want to hear anything bad. Don't tell me that you are here because François is dead.

She replied to me saying that François is very sick, but he wants to see me at any cost.

Ok let me take a quick shower then we can go to the Hospital.

As we arrived I took a chair and sat close to him. I ask him what was wrong with him. He told me that one of his coworker put a poison in his drunk during the party at their work place.

<I don't know if I can make it that why I called you. I want to set my eyes on you for the last time.

What you talking about François? Don't even tell me such of things. You will make it.

Do you remember when we went to see the native Doctor for the solution of our problem?

Yes love François I remember. The way he reacted toward us front of everybody was strange I really did not like it.

I just want to forget about the past, those brutal memories, but François kept talking saying this:

<See baby girl, now I realize that the native Doctor was right telling us a He knew that something bad will happen to me in a future and you will be left alone with our kids as a young widow>

As he was talking I started crying telling him that I would have choose to be a widow with his kids than be who I'm now. At least I would have been happy with him till now. I have faith François that you will be head soon. You don't have to give up on us now Francois because your wife and your kids need you they are too young and your family relies on you can't you see it?

I know love my beauty queen as I always call you. I know that I have no power over my destiny.

How I wish that I can turn the clock back. I would have be very careful and avoid what is happening to me now my Queen. Time can never tell us when the wind can blow for our turn to leave this world.

If that happen to me today or in few days, remember my Queen that I will go happily because I saw before living. I know it wasn't the will of God for me and you to be husband and wife that why.

I want to confess something to you Francois. I did not intended to leave you that day, but my family told me that they put a spell on me through the peanut that we all eat in order to change my mind toward you.

I knew that something was wrong somewhere didn't I say that. It was so obvious that you changed your mind and your attitude toward me for no reason. That is ok I will not blame them for what is happening to me right now, I can forgive them. Our destiny did not cross that all.

Since twelve years we have been separated because of Vincent, but I still always love you. I carry your love inside of me forever. The love that I have for you will never died. It will be always with me even if I leave you, put it in your mind that I love you and I will always love you.>

I want you not to forget about me through your life time. No matter what you do I will always be there for you. Men will love you, but you will not feel that love as you felt mine. You should never let anybody put you down for what you are. Love because your heart is telling you to love, but not because of well being of the person that you want to love. Be always with my family members pay them visit if you can. You are a smart woman I will pray for you for a good marriage in your life. Time will come that you will meet someone who will have my spirit to love you the way that I did. You will feel it when that moment comes. Your good heart will carry you through life. Everybody will not pay you back for the good that you do for them, but your reward will soon or later come back to you. You have a daughter how old is she?

She is only six months I left her home when I was coming to see you.

I know that she is beautiful as you are. She is my daughter too even if you did not have her with me.

Is Vincent her father?

No her father is from Dabou met him in BURKINA FASSO couple years ago.

He is good to you?

Yes, but he is married and has some other kids. My daughter is the last of his children.

We talk about everything that we could than he told me to help him to sit at the edge of the bed.

We ate the meal that his wife brought to him. I use that moment to meet her and have a conversation with her. She said to me that Francois still have my pictures and those that he and I took on a wall of their house.

It was nice to see you again. The first time that I saw you was at my father's work place. After you left Francois, my father decided to married me to him. We have two kids one boys and one girl.

Oh thanks for taking care of him little sister I said to her.

You welcome she replied.

I spent half of the day with him, but because of my baby that I left home I have to go back.

Thanks for coming my Queen. Help me to get back to bed and you can go later.

Few hours later François felt as sleep. I did not want to wake him up, but he opens his eyes and told me goodbye. I knelt down to kiss him and said bye to him.

I see later and take care of yourself he said to me.

That shot period of time that we stay together was my last time to see Francois a life.

The next day I got a message from my mom that I should go to see Francois's family.

Mom I was with François yesterday at the hospital. Why are you telling me this?

I just have a feeling that you should visit them that all.

Ok I will be on my way after couple hours.

I got dress and went to the bus station as soon as possible. As I was going to take the bus, my heart was beating faster and faster. I don't know why. I felt as if I was chocking.

Soon I reached François family's house, one of his niece came to me and took me and surround me with some other family members. What is going on here? Where was François I asked him?

Everybody started crying. I felt on a ground and lost conscience. I don't know how long, but when I woke up all my cloth was wet of cool water that they did pour on me.

After few hours of crying, I went to his wife and ask her what did happen when I left the hospital.

She told me that soon I left the hospital he told her that he wanted to sleep and he didn't want anybody to disturb him. He told her that he will not eat again for the rest of the day.

She said to him that it was early to sleep now, but he replied saying that he really wanted to sleep.

He slept and in the middle of the night she tried to wake him up, but he never woke up. He was already dead.

I stay with François family all day long and went home at night fall. Before I left the funeral place I told everybody the dream that I had about him, the conversation that him and I had, and what the native Doctor told us about our getting married. I felt in my heart such of pain as if someone stabbed me in a chest.

It was a wound inside of me now after years I feel it. My heart bled when she was telling me how François died. I felt inside of me such of fast heart beating and a squeezing pain from my chest to my throat. My wound had just reopened and it will never be healed again so his. I cannot replace what had been taken away from me. I also cannot give back what I had taken from François.

I cannot turn the clock back to fix what had been destroy. I always try to forget about those crucial moment of my youth life, but it make believe sometimes that I don't need a man to live my life.

We can never tell what can happen to us one day. When, how, where, and if so, what will we do to fix our past. I think that we should always follow how heart no matter how. Destiny sometimes cannot tell us what our future will be like. We just need to give ourselves a credit for a life gift.